THE HANDBOOK OF
FIELD
MARKETING

THE HANDBOOK OF
FIELD
MARKETING

A complete guide to understanding and
outsourcing face-to-face direct marketing

Alison Williams & Roddy Mullin

KOGAN
PAGE

London and Philadelphia

Publisher's note

Every possible effort has been made to ensure that the information contained in this book is accurate at the time of going to press, and the publishers and authors cannot accept responsibility for any errors or omissions, however caused. No responsibility for loss or damage occasioned to any person acting, or refraining from action, as a result of the material in this publication can be accepted by the editor, the publisher or either of the authors.

First published in Great Britain and the United States in 2008 by Kogan Page Limited

120 Pentonville Road
London N1 9JN
United Kingdom
www.kogan-page.co.uk

525 South 4th Street, #241
Philadelphia PA 19147
USA

© Alison Williams and Roddy Mullin, 2008

ISBN 978 0 7494 5025 0

British Library Cataloguing-in-Publication Data

A CIP record for this book is available from the British Library.

Library of Congress Cataloging-in-Publication Data

Williams, Alison.
    The handbook of field marketing : a complete guide to understanding and outsourcing face-to-face direct marketing / Alison Williams and Roddy Mullin.
        p. cm.
    Includes index.
    ISBN 978-0-7494-5025-0
    1. Direct marketing. 2. Sales promotion. 3. Sampling. 4. Branding (Marketing) I. Mullin, Roddy. II. Title.
    HF5415.126.W55 2007
    658.8'72--dc22

                        2007037070

Typeset by Saxon Graphics Ltd, Derby
Printed and bound in Great Britain by MPG Books Ltd, Bodmin, Cornwall

Contents

List of case studies

Foreword

It was during my Chairmanship of the Direct Marketing Association (DMA) that the Field Marketing Association joined us to add field marketing to the ever-growing channel options available to direct marketing professionals.

Until that time the term field marketing was something of an unknown to me but Alison Williams as the chair of the newly formed Field Marketing Council with a subsequent seat on the DMA Board began to vex my curiosity with her obvious knowledge and enthusiasm for her industry sector.

I think what surprised me most of all was the multiple disciplines which are included in field marketing. I had heard of them all, of course; the stimulation of sales, merchandising, auditing, sampling and demonstrating, mystery calling and shopping, and experiential marketing. I had experience in some of them, but it had never occurred to me that all these disciplines combined came under the singular banner of field marketing and were available en masse from suppliers like Alison's company FDS.

Alison, never slow to react to a willing pupil, schooled me and many others at the DMA and I found myself wanting to know more and more about this untapped direct marketing channel and I now constantly draw my clients' attention to the power of face-to-face marketing.

I introduced Roddy Mullin to Alison at a Masterclass I had organized for the Worshipful Company of Marketors, an organization to which I belong, thanks to my nomination by two of my marketing heroes, Roddy and Judith

Donovan, CBE. I had asked Alison to speak about field marketing and she had given one of her virtuoso presentations.

The next thing I hear is that Roddy and Alison have decided to write a book together on field marketing. The dream team, no less, writing a much-needed guide to an underused direct marketing channel.

And here it is, and I feel privileged to be the first to read it. The book is an easy to understand, no-nonsense guide with in-depth coverage of the principles of the building blocks of field marketing followed by practical examples of how to use the various disciplines to deliver, for example, a mouth-watering return on investment or an impressive increase in brand share.

At a time when consumers are time-pressured and have a low attention span, Alison and Roddy have demonstrated with real examples that field marketing can provide a method of breaking through the clutter to capture their attention whether for short- or long-term goals, and they have demystified the processes brilliantly.

The well-kept secret of the power of field marketing is now out in the open, as readers of this book will soon find out.

Jenny Moseley
Former Chairman, DMA

Preface

Customers are changing the way they buy. Businesses, organizations and especially retail have a saviour – field marketing (FM).

FM offers an awesome return, as the case studies, reasoning and practices suggested in this book will show. It is how you get ahead of the customers, whether consumers or clients, as they change the way they buy in the 21st century and as the internet gains prominence. FM can be applied in business, by charities, by member bodies and in the public sector. FM is often applied at the point of sale (POS) to support the purchase decision, for it also penetrates the mind of the customer, thus making it a powerful way to provide brand experience, to imbue brand values and increase brand loyalty, for future and referral purchases. As well as the amazing return (detailed later, in examples), it is estimated that 15 per cent can be saved by outsourcing the sales function. That calculation has to include, quite reasonably, the money that a company would spend or have spent in-house in support of the sales field team, ie on payroll, HR, fleet support, administration, desks, light, heat, space, etc. By outsourcing FM, it also removes the worry of sales for a client. As a consequence of the benefits – no worries, savings on costs and improved business (selling more and growing the brand) – there is an understandable natural aversion to passing on information generally about FM. But the authors think there is enough here to more than whet the appetite. The authors believe that FM should be used much more widely, particularly to overcome customer resistance; that FM should be tested by the more cynical, applying FM for a specific venture to experience the real benefits of FM at first hand (and the authors even offer help here to those who only want to dabble in FM a little, in-house).

Trading in the UK over the Christmas period 2006 was disastrous for retailers – the worst since records began in 1986. Figures indicate both a small volume decrease of 1.8 per cent in January 2007 over the previous month coupled with a discounting of 33.7 per cent on goods sold in January 2007 over December 2006; in other words, discounting – even at that level – did not persuade consumers to buy. The impact on retailers was dire (although the situation did improve the next month).

Not all was doom and gloom for everyone, as some did OK. (Perhaps they were FM users.) Also, the internet saw a 17.7 per cent sales growth. So what does a proactive retailer do, apart from establishing a decent website to match the growing online preference of customers? First why not try to find out how the few did well? The case studies in this book indicate how astute companies were using FM at the time of writing (in May 2007) and how others, who follow their example, might restore sales' fortunes. But who are these clever firms using FM? A quick check of the client lists and case studies of FM agencies (enter 'field marketing' into a search engine to find them) provides the names.

Dealing with the cynical customer

The counter to customer cynicism with marketing

FM provides a very real solution for companies, particularly those averse to discounting. FM matches customers' needs in the 21st century to experience the brand, to establish a relationship with the brand and to establish in their minds a perceived yet very real value of the brand. The cynicism of consumers is real; advertising is failing because consumers have seen it all before. People feel they are intelligent and better informed and they have increased competency – they use the internet, for example – and they want to be interacted with and engaged through communication matched to their level and preference. FM accommodates this new customer behaviour. Marketing used to be about telling but this must be changed to the new marketing, which reasons and persuades. For consumers, the buying process (described in Chapter 1) is about finding information, as they search for and define their needs, then look for suppliers and seek verification and validation of that information, before making a purchase decision. Instant gratification is the aim rather than drawn out negotiation, as they try to get answers. FM is best placed to deal with this as it engages with consumers providing real-time answers at the POS when consumers – the customers – need support for their decision to purchase.

Customers are changing the way they buy

How are customers changing the way they buy? Buying on-line is becoming huge, as the Christmas 2006 figures show. The internet is convenient. It is widely available in the home and at internet cafés and it is often a cheaper way to buy than in-store. Online turnover at John Lewis now beats turnover at their biggest store. Surveys in the run-up to Christmas 2006 indicated that 50 per cent of purchases made by many consumers are through websites. How are businesses reacting? Argos is offering a buy online, collect from store service; but many other stores reported poor trading and issued profit warnings.

But the internet does not have it all for the customer, unless it leads to a rare website – figleaves.com is a good example. Most websites do not deliver any brand relationship or matched communication between the brand and the potential customer. People like to experience the brand. So how have people changed to accommodate this? People may use retail browsing, where they look first in shops at what they want to buy – called retail therapy by some – looking for products or services or a mix of both, but then they use the internet, sometimes via specialist websites that list all suppliers, to purchase online. An example of these websites is pricerunner.com. Even then people still prefer to buy from a recognized supplier or purchase a recognized brand. People do like to build a relationship with a brand.

So how do you ensure that your brand is recognized, that customers are aware of your branded item and how then do they build a relationship with your brand in the internet age? You can do it in large part through FM, which is described, illustrated and demonstrated in this book.

Customers are now really aware of marketing

There is increasing real knowledge and a general sagacity of customers in their approach to and perception of marketing. This applies whether the customer is at that time acting as a business person or a consumer or as a member of the public or a member of a professional body. Customers now know when they are on to a good thing. For example, over the Christmas 2006 period Threshers ran a sales promotion that seemed to be too good to be true offering a large discount. The word spread and a 60 per cent volume increase resulted – but with Thresher still reporting a profit and a massive database of new customers. The jury is out on whether it was intended or not and whether it was good for Threshers. Certainly though, consumers flocked to the offer. It was not FM but shows how savvy customers have become.

What else affects people? There are two things that are presently dominating people's lives: time and quality of life. Time is becoming precious and for routine activities such as commodity shopping, people are prepared to forego the need to examine competitor products or outlets. Customers bond with a brand to the exclusion of others, and that brand must offer quality and convenience at an acceptable value level. In 2001 43 per cent of the top third (ie high spending) Tesco customers did not bother to think of shopping anywhere else. Tesco, of course, is into FM in a big way. Time has also affected products: products that are ready to use, plug in and play, take away, drive away, or ready to eat are all now big earners – and for all of these, FM can be the trigger to selection and purchase through sampling, demonstrating, highly targeted sales, experiential marketing, road shows and events.

To achieve quality of life means customers consciously assess and select products and services that improve lifestyle against personal criteria. This is seen in some advertising messages: 'Go on, spoil yourself, you're worth it', tempting consumers to go for that perceived rise in quality of life. A particular product or service may cost more, but if it is part of or adds to a person's quality of life, that person's perceived preferred image of himself or herself, then the customer is prepared to pay; there is no need to discount – indeed that would remove the customer's preferred expensive, exclusive cachet. This is particularly true for traditional buying-as-gifts retail sectors such as jewellery, where there is a strong move to purchases made by individuals for their own use. FM has a part to play here in delivering the glitz, encouraging people to sample, to experience and particularly succumb to a strategic or tactical or one-off sales campaign.

It is also true that customers have developed an immunity to advertisements generally, probably only noticing those that are offensive (which can backfire on the advertiser), those that offer humour (but that may not make them remember the product or service) and those that offer a brand they recognize, which reinforces their brand awareness and brand experience. If you don't believe that people have become immune to a lot of advertising, ask anyone to recall from a recently read magazine or newspaper, any advertisements. People may recall one and probably only one that is relevant to them. Something different is needed. That something is FM.

Yet some businesses still ignore the customer

Why is it important to consider the customer? Because the customer brings in the money, the revenue, and that pays the costs and generates the profit.

More than that, customers have a choice; they can purchase from a competitor or any supplier or choose an indirect solution. There is thus a requirement to understand why they choose to buy from one supplier rather than another. Suppliers can then use that knowledge to gain that customer preferential edge. In order to communicate with customers, their communication needs to be understood too and communication matched to their preference.

If your customer, such as a business to business (B2B) firm, has its own customers then you must understand both levels of customer. In the experience of one of the authors this is not always really comprehended or believed. Not only is there a view among some businesses that their customers' views do not matter, but worse, assumptions are made about customers that are quite invalid or way off the truth. They do not carry out any research into why their customers buy. Even where research is carried out the findings are not accepted or responded to (estate agents and property developers are prone to this). This is particularly true of professional bodies in which one author has served. Businesses and organizations that ignore the customer deserve to fail.

The FM difference

Why does FM have the edge?

FM can be differentiated from all other direct marketing activities because it is face-to-face personal contact direct marketing. FM includes highly targeted direct selling promotions, merchandising, auditing, sampling and demonstration, experiential marketing, organizing road shows, events and mystery shopping. These disciplines, individually or combined, develop brands and in their implementation show a clear real return on investment (ROI) to the brand owner. This is a key feature and benefit of FM – seeing revenue expenditure generate a specific return.

FM is an industry worth an estimated £770 million per year in the UK alone (according to the DMA Census of Marketing, 2005). The disciplines of FM have been around for decades, but because it is a relatively new consolidation of all the activities of face-to-face marketing, it does not yet feature on the academic radar, so there is little awareness of these disciplines. There is no book on FM in print. The arrival of the first retail academy in late summer 2006 indicates a recognition of the importance of FM.

In December 2006 *Marketing Week* (Parker, 2006) forecast that alongside digital media (text, e-mail), event and experiential marketing is going to be the next marketing growth area. Event marketing is described as a 'now media' star. It allows the consumer to build a relationship beyond what is achievable online or in any other media. TV channels (the BBC, Channel 4), a software owner (Microsoft) or mobile phone supplier (Motorola) all offer events for consumers to attend. This allows the consumer to experience the brand at first hand – which is why it is also called experiential marketing. Experiential marketing is one part of one of the six disciplines of FM.

Using FM disciplines is really powerful, as behind FM lies the key face-to-face principle that commonsense and research show brings in sales and profits. It is no use spending a fortune on promoting a brand through advertising, PR or the non-face-to-face parts of direct marketing, unless you ensure that brand delivery occurs at the POS. If you have obtained ownership of part of the mind of a potential customer at some expense, do not throw that away at the POS. FM, through sampling, demonstrating and operating experiential events, powerfully reinforces the brand at the POS, merchandising ensures the agreed product display occurs and the audit confirms that it happens, even when no one from the supplier is there. Mystery calling and mystery shopping also play a part to see whether training has been implemented and worked. Ongoing projects, short-term projects and a mix of both types for specific sales campaigns are the ways that FM disciplines are implemented to offer near pinpoint targeting accuracy – the opposite of a scatter-gun approach to marketing.

At the start of 2007, *Marketing Week* reported (Parker, 2006) that exhibitions with attendance dropping 25 per cent over the period 1998 to 2005 – stuck in a 'shell-scheme hell' – should eventually realize that by becoming event-based they may see a revival. What that means is: food exhibitions become taste events, motor shows offer driving experience, skiing is practised at ski shows. The new Manchester Virgin Megastore boasts an auditorium for 250 people and showcases live performances. There is also a testing area where shoppers can try out products on offer. So it is FM that provides a solution to revive the flagging exhibition world.

Can you use FM disciplines without using an FM agency as a contracted partner?

The authors have spent a lot of time discussing this question. The answer is technically 'no' if the definition of FM is taken as including outsourcing to an FM agency. If it covers all in-house FM involves, it should illustrate why outsourcing the sales function is preferable. Contractual, professional, dedicated, experienced, customer-matched, highly trained sales face-to-face activity – that is a different matter. So the authors have included guidance for in-house face-to-face activity for a broader FM completeness. In any case FM teams are generally more likely to achieve better sales face to face than in-house staff. In-house face-to-face activities are so poorly carried out both in store and at exhibitions that there is a desperate need to improve them. If Christmas 2006 was such a disaster for retail as described above, then poor in-house sales training must be in part to blame. Retailers should have turned to FM, either outsourcing or using in-house sales training by FM staff, or applying the third but weaker option of DIY for which the authors give guidance at the end of the book.

One of the two authors, by applying the DIY option for example, has assisted clients improve sales by 22 per cent directly to the bottom line, through applying a small amount of highly targeted sales training. Another manufacturing client's staff was recently trained in October 2006 to focus on the customer. The client won enough new business from existing customers that, although it was out of season when sales normally drop, the company returned to full production and postponed sales activity to prospect for new clients until later in 2007, when more production comes on stream. Another client in a professional services sector has achieved a brand position within the top three in its sector, after previously being 'in the noise', all because marketing and sales training of the whole staff towards a particular client prospect type was truly beneficial. Another client took training focused on how to sell at exhibitions. Now, at exhibitions, the company routinely takes three and a half times more orders in terms of value than before and is successful – even when stands all around report 'a poor exhibition'. In fact two clients are so embarrassed by the poor performance at Top Drawer, the Spring Fair, etc. in stands around them that they pleaded that this face-to-face book should give some guidance to help others and so overcome their embarrassment. Training of in-house staff by suppliers' clients is a regular part of the sales call, typically for a new product launch.

So for face-to-face completeness, although not strictly part of FM, this book touches on in-house face-to-face contact with the customer, including selling at exhibitions, because these activities also deliver face-to-face brand awareness and brand delivery at the POS (see Chapter 19). This is guidance, no more, towards the standard achieved by staff in FM agencies. A supplier seeking to go further should ask the FM agency for in-house staff training and finally outsource the sales function. However, the attempt here to raise in-house standards, from the insights in Chapter 19, should assist with understanding, by extrapolation, of just how powerful FM is.

FM – bang and whiz – without discounting

So FM is raising awareness, experience and delivery of the brand at the POS. FM makes the brand come alive. A successful brand owns a space in a customer's mind and FM is one way to place it there, fast, correctly and at a high level of priority over any other brand held in the mind. It helps in winning the battle of the brands in the mind. FM does this through a toolbox of disciplines that you should mix and match to meet the marketing objectives. Like sales promotions, FM can supply fun, excitement and interest at the POS, but whereas sales promotions often directly adversely affects the bottom line, FM retains the price and with that, a key element of the brand's value. If your brand is perceived as an expensive product or service then you want it to remain so and you need a means so that you do not to have to resort to discounting; FM can do this.

Applying FM in non-retail sectors – the business to persons (B2P) arena

Clearly FM is suited to retail. It can also be extended fairly logically to B2B as this book will demonstrate. What about other organizations and non-retail businesses? Here the authors want to describe a further use for FM – you read it here first – B2P (the persons being, for example, professionals, members of institutions, single-person businesses, the self-employed). FM can be applied here just as anywhere else where marketing is used.

Take a professional body for example, say an engineering-based institution that finds its revenue forecast from membership is insufficient to cover predicted costs. It needs income from non-member-based activity such as selling training and specialist courses, publications and offering professional advice both to members and other professionals (B2P) – particularly nowadays to government and the agencies that have taken over parts of government. The institution staff needs to have the brand imbued in them as a culture and the institution websites have to be designed with the identified target audiences in mind, but as brand deliverers – brand ambassadors in FM terms – the staff reaction at the POS is really important. Using FM disciplines, a mystery caller can confirm how they (as a B2P) are dealt with by the institution staff and report back to confirm that the culture and responses are appropriate to the target audiences sought. When members attend events, perhaps having been enticed to attend events for free, FM disciplines can be employed to provide experience of and sell-in the benefits of training, courses, publications and professional advice, face-to-face (to B2Ps). The same applies to charities. Bombarding potential donors with competing tales of woe is no solution. The consumer is becoming saturated by disaster. To be different a charity needs to offer initially free brand (or cause) experience to obtain and hold a place in the mind of the donor (the charity's B2P). FM does just this.

The authors believe that FM applies in the public sector too, where presently there is too much reliance on the media to report back and often with the wrong spin, serving no one well. An example is HM Revenue & Customs who wisely now offer free 'meet the staff/training days on VAT' to self-employed persons (their B2P). The Armed Services have always recognized the benefits of open days. But these in-house events could of course be much strengthened using professional FM agencies.

The arrival of integration, the new media and new technology

Marketing integration has arrived

Integrated marketing, which in this book means including FM in the overall marketing process, seeks to move the customer along from knowing nothing about a product or service, to eventually making the purchase, then willingly repeating the purchase thereafter. Marketing integration produces consistency of communication. Research by Professor Merlin Stone shows that it can save 30 per cent of 'lost' sales arising from the differences between the marketing promise, the selling conditions and the operational reality of the service provided. At Virgin One Account one of the authors found this fault caused 30 per cent customer loss after 13 weeks. The brand message must be consistent. The sales staff at Virgin One also did not match the target audience – a further problem, but one that FM shows is important. FM takes a pride in matching its practitioners – the brand ambassadors – to the target audience.

A campaign by agency SPF15 in 2006 saw Superdrug increase its favourable brand awareness from 15 to 33 per cent with 170,000 women signed up (to the detriment of a major high street competitor). This campaign is an example of both a sequential and an integrated approach, and one where a number of businesses joined in partnership. SPF15 leveraged the important special 'little moment' (to her, the target customer) of a woman preparing to go on holiday, using advertising, texts, mail (sending out a pack) and e-mail. The result made 25 per cent of the participants 'feel special' and 38 per cent recorded that the campaign reached them at the perfect time, with the result that 27 per cent now 'love Superdrug' and 42 per cent are 'feeling better about Superdrug'. An example of creative, innovative, integrated brand building.

New media and technology

A lot of changes have affected the environment in which marketing exists. First, there are new media (the internet, text messaging and interactive TV) to consider as additional channels. Remember some customers are now never more than a few centimetres (or 6 inches) from their mobile or 'blackberry'.

Second, the new technology is making life both more complex but once mastered, easier. There are third generation mobile phones; powerful and affordable PCs, laptops and hand-held devices, with their associated peripherals, software and interoperability; digital cameras and rapid electronic transmission of images – all readily accessible and affordable. Marketers have to understand the formats favoured and used in these communication channels.

FM is benefiting too from the new technology. An audit can take seconds to carry out – providing evidence in moments. Measurement and accountability (see Chapter 14), acknowledges that the marketer now has to offer value for money for all marketing activities within the business or organization. 'Revenue expenditure' is a new skill that will eventually equal traditional cost expenditure in importance; analysing the return on the marketing investment for the benefit obtained. FM is most suited to revenue expenditure analysis as the FM techniques all include built-in accountability.

The web as a source of information

The web allows you, the reader, to keep right up to date. The text refers to websites to allow you to access the latest thinking, examples and case studies. Research for another book shows that people still value case studies, which is why some are included here.

Overview of the book

Who needs this book?

In consequence of its uniqueness, this book should be an immediate winner with a number of readers. These include: anyone in retail seeking an alternative to discounting; charities and non-profit organizations who want to offer a different approach to improve revenue generation; those in the public sector seeking to engage minds. Indeed the book should be a immediate winner with anyone in marketing or those who employ marketers, and with students on marketing and sales courses, not only because it is the only one focused on FM but because it also shows how all the parts of FM fit in with the rest of direct marketing and marketing itself. It will be of equal benefit to anyone directly employing anyone as FM staff or the FM people themselves, whether they are demonstrators, merchandisers, mystery shoppers or salespersons – the brand ambassadors, who will find it really beneficial to understanding FM and how to be better at it, learning from the lessons of the case studies and the many tips included in the text. It will finally help businesses that intend to undertake FM, whether they want to update their FM activities or are starting a new business.

The authors

The authors of the book offer complementary experience and expertise. Alison Williams has chaired the FM Industry Association for over 12 years and is the (first) Chairman of the DMA Field Marketing Council, and a Board Member of the DMA. She has been involved with FM in all its facets for 25 years through her own company of which she is now Chairman. Roddy Mullin is a chartered marketer bringing an overview of how FM fits in to the rest of marketing, who has helped clients over 20 years sell in shops, sell to businesses, sell to win at pitches for contracts and take orders at exhibitions (it is his clients who plead with him each year to improve the pitiful performance of competitors at both the Spring Fair and Top Drawer and are so embarrassed with the reportedly poor sales performance of others at those events); Roddy has increased orders at exhibitions near fourfold year on year. Roddy's wife Pam was a merchandiser for 10 years and they have jointly 'mystery shopped'. Roddy Mullin is also the author of other 'how to' marketing books for Kogan Page (see the 'Further information' section).

What the book does

This book will allow a person with a specific interest in FM to understand, within the context of marketing as a whole, how to undertake FM without having to learn from their own mistakes.

Other benefits covered in this book include the following:

- The context of FM is explained within an integrated marketing approach, when strategy considerations favour FM and how FM is used in support of the brand.
- The context of marketing as a whole includes:
  - an analysis of the customer in the 21st century and the importance of market research to find out customers' buying behaviour and their buying process in order to establish a sales process;
  - getting the offer (the marketing mix) right in terms of the six Cs: cost, convenience, concept, communication, customer relationship and consistency (the customer view of the four Ps: the product or service, the place, the price, the promotion);
  - communicating and promoting the offer to the customer through channels that they use and using the language with which they are familiar in order to communicate and promote messages successfully to them.
- To illustrate the points made in the text, many examples are given in easy-to-find case studies. Tips are also given.
- The law and FM is outlined, including employment and health and safety law.
- International FM is explored with considerations on how to achieve it.
- The book also deals with measuring FM and its success with the use of ROI criteria (revenue expenditure analysis) that will measure the payback to the clients from the marketing investment they have made. FM has some of the best ROI in the marketing industry. Be aware that the FM jargon is industry-related and does not necessarily conform to academic accountancy terminology.
- The use of technology in FM to give real-time reporting and instant web access to results is also covered.

The layout of this book

The first part of the book looks at all the issues that FM practitioners should consider.

FM is seen as a part of the whole marketing effort, making its contribution in a consistent manner to build the brand. FM has come of age in that it is now accepted that it has a role to play in overall marketing, and operates within legal constraints and codes of practice. In the past it was seen as 'separate'. What FM can achieve and how the disciplines of FM can be implemented are dealt with in this book. The importance of creativity is touched on along with ideas which can be picked up from the case studies.

The second part of the book deals with practice techniques. To avoid repetition, international FM, whether in one or many countries, appears in one part only. Given the speed at which examples can date, sources of recent examples, such as the annual FM awards, are included.

Reference is made to websites where up-to-date codes of practice, the law relating to FM, and examples can be found. Reference is also made to other books dealing with topics that impact on FM, such as creativity, controlling agencies and more on marketing accountability (justifying marketing spend or revenue expenditure as it is becoming known).

Acknowledgements

The authors would like to thank friends and colleagues in the business, particularly Alison's fellow directors and colleagues throughout the FDS Group who kept us on the straight and narrow and clients of Roddy's own business, Helmsmen Business Consultants, who had a lot to say.

Comment

On a personal note, we'd like to say how much we have enjoyed the opportunity to prepare this book. Roddy doubts he will ever acquire as much knowledge as Alison has on the subject of FM but he hopes he has put the subject into the context of mainstream marketing. We hope this complementary approach will help you to put leading edge FM as part of your practitioner's toolbox.

We have spent much time looking at case studies selecting only those that really help. We stress the benefit of using the web to see other examples.

We can but commend the reader to this new book, the first ever on field marketing.

Alison Williams
Roddy Mullin

Introduction

The FM 'toolkit' differentiates the successful business and especially the retailer, from the unsuccessful.

FM disciplines are not well understood by marketers, nor are the improvement, difference and value that applying FM disciplines can give to a brand. Any student with a marketing degree will probably never have heard of FM – as it has yet to be discovered by the academics – yet FM has been available for 40 years or more. The sector continues to grow to fulfil the FM needs of those businesses clever enough to have discovered it.

FM is the crème de la crème of sales, which is why it is inherently successful and why it is the antidote to discounting and the flag bearer of brand awareness and brand growth.

What FM is, the FM disciplines and what FM does

History of FM

FM can trace its origins back to the 1930s when independent retailers were still a major force in British retailing and the novel idea of self-service had yet to hatch.

Consequently, there were a few small companies that would visit these outlets on behalf of manufacturers to leverage the valuable space on the counter over which all products were served. Placement in the prime position on the counter invariably led to increased impulse purchases, an entity that has now come full circle as placement compliance is a key FM task.

With the development of the major multiple supermarkets like Tesco and Sainsbury that grew rapidly during the 1960s and 1970s, the emphasis switched towards representation at store level. This led to the establishment of four companies providing merchandisers, tactical sales forces and sampling, to take compliance and other face-to-face activities, now associated with FM, forward into the supermarket self-service arena.

It was in the late 1970s that the multiples introduced planograms, which reduced the opportunity to negotiate for space locally; this also resulted in a shift towards more sales-related activities. Also during this time, the number of manufacturers turning to outsourced sales and merchandising teams increased as so too has the number of FM companies to take up the work generated.

The services of the industry further developed into auditing, mystery shopping and event management and large outsourcing contracts became common between the major FMCG manufacturers and FM companies. As the FM industry diversified to encompass more disciplines, the emphasis moved back to the independent sector. Manufacturers realized that this sector still had a significant contribution to make in terms of volume and profit.

A further milestone in the industry came in 1997 with the deregulation of utilities, and FM moved to doorstep selling. This activity alone is estimated to have contributed in excess of £40 million to the industry. (Source: *Users' Guide to Field Marketing* prepared by the Field Marketing Council (FMC): see www.dma.org.uk)

Currently, the FM companies have focused more on doing the work more professionally with the introduction of sophisticated technology and reporting systems that lead to greater flexibility, productivity and ROI for the client. There is a noticeable shift of focus too in parts of the industry from the retailer to the consumer.

Definitions

The Direct Marketing Association (DMA) – the body that brings together all the major FM practitioners in the UK through the FMC – gives this definition of FM:

> It is the provision of highly trained and skilfully managed staff to conduct brand-building activities on behalf of a client. These staff work for the FM

company, which in turn is outsourced by the client to meet specific goals and targets. The staff used will interact, explain, shock, assist or pacify and, above all, give feedback to the client whilst developing his brand in line with his brand strategies, and nurturing his brand with CRM that is specific, targeted and measurable. All FM activities give measurable results with a clearly defined return on investment.

The *Users' Guide to Field Marketing* (see www.dma.org.uk) has a shorter alternative: 'field marketing is the function of outsourcing sales and promotional activities, which are conducted by professionals and audited strictly in terms of results'.

The FMC has also used: 'field marketing is measurable, face-to-face brand development and customer relationship management through using highly trained people'.

All the definitions are somewhat circular stating in other words that FM activities are carried out by FM companies, which although strictly true does not explain the face-to-face element or highlight the ROI benefits or the brand experience or delivery of brand values.

The authors might venture a further definition:

> Field marketing is the outsourcing of a sales or marketing project to direct, face-to-face marketing which explains, educates and influences the customer to affect future purchasing decisions, either ongoing or as a short-term fix. The outsourcing of this function to highly trained staff, specializing in delivering brand experience, brand values and sales, allows flexibility of budget and releases the client to focus on his core business. FM is highly measurable in terms of ROI.

And the authors describe what FM does and how and when to use it, as: 'FM focuses the attention on a particular product, at a particular time, at the POS when customer behaviour with regard to awareness and experience of the brand can be influenced'.

The Direct Marketing Association (DMA)

The DMA is the largest marketing trade body in Europe, and second in the world to the US DMA. The DMA is the organization that is the guardian of the consumers' interests and the direct marketing industry. The organization has association with many differing trade bodies, government agencies and the government itself. Many different direct marketing disciplines are part of the DMA, and are represented by councils. FM is represented within the DMA, where the Field Marketing Council (FMC) is the industry body. This is the perfect place for FM to sit; after all nothing is more direct than putting a person in front of an end user!

The Field Marketing Council (FMC)

The FMC has a vision statement, a mission and offers best practice guidelines:

> VISION: To achieve widespread brand owner recognition of the value and the importance of FM for the personal expression of their brands.
>
> MISSION: Our mission is to ensure that FMC members operate to the highest professional standards producing the best possible project outcomes, making FMC members the automatic first choice for every client.

Best practice guidelines

The FMC best practice guidelines, together with the DMA codes of conduct, set the standards for entry to the FMC. All FM companies who apply to join the FMC are visited and checked against the standards before being admitted to membership. There are currently 30 members of the FMC; two applicants have been rejected for not meeting the required standard.

Basic principles of the FMC best practice guidelines

The basic principles are as follows:

- All activities need to be legal, decent, honest and truthful.
- Every activity should be carried out with a due sense of social responsibility.
- No activity should be carried out so as to impair confidence in FM.
- All activities should conform to the principles of fair competition as generally accepted in business, in particular with regard to:
  - the terms of the offer, including price and modes of payment, and the methods and form of the contact with the consumer;
  - the method of presentation and demonstration of the product;
  - the fulfilment of any obligation arising from the offer or any operation connected with it.
- FM companies should voluntarily assume responsibility towards the consumer with respect to fair sales methods, product value and product information and should make every effort to ensure consumer satisfaction.
- FM companies should also make a commitment to their responsibility for the field employees.
- FM companies should be fully briefed by the client or agency as to the characteristics of the goods and services offered, to enable them to

provide the target audience with the information they are likely to need.

- Every activity should be carried out with a due sense of social responsibility, inspiring trust and confidence. FM personnel must act in an ethical and professional manner, showing due sensitivity for consumers' time constraints.

The industry is one that employs an estimated 40,000 people, and adherence to the law, sound processes and high ethics are important in an FM company. The DMA standards are important, and must apply.

Over and above these standards, the FMC have written an accreditation scheme. This is a 'super standard' that members can attain, and requires a visit to the member by an independent body, to ensure that this 'super standard' is regular practice in the member agency. The scheme was devised to drive the standards in FM even higher.

Some agencies, usually small ones that are run from a back room, are able to offer low prices, as they have no overheads related to offices and staff, but they do not all offer the level of service that would be expected by a client. It would be advisable for a client wanting FM to check that the agency they are planning to recruit is able to deliver the job in hand. Of course a member of the FMC will be able to deliver, and a list of these members can be found on the DMA website on www.dma.org.uk.

Investors in People (IiP)

IiP is a standard that relates to the development and improvement in the staff within a company and as an FM company is a people business IiP is virtually a prerequisite. IiP, once achieved, is revisited at regular intervals (usually every two years) to see that the company is moving forward in developing its staff. These IiP visits are very helpful to the company, not only are they confirming that it is moving forward in staff relations and development, but also give suggestions and ideas of how systems could be improved further. Every FM company should have IiP accreditation.

The FMC overview of FM

After stating that 'field marketing is measurable, face-to-face brand development and customer relationship management through using highly trained people' the FMC continues:

FM builds the brand face-to-face by giving brand experience of the product or service, often one-on-one to the potential customer, while developing a relationship associated with the brand at the same time – a personalization of the brand – such that the customers are persuaded to purchase. The FMC highlight the benefits as measurable ROI, the excellence of the staff and the high standards of operation/ethics set.

A key benefit of almost all FM activities is that they give measurable results with a clearly defined ROI. The exception is experiential FM work; but ideas on how to make experiential work accountable are included in Chapter 14. ROI and the accountability of marketing are becoming growing business needs. Investment in face-to-face marketing can now be shown to bring in a better return than other marketing activities. Brand owners can now see real-time reporting through the use of hand-held terminals and wireless technology and learn how to leverage in-store presence. FM perhaps needs to finally prove the link to ROI, fully and incontrovertibly, to remove all doubts about its power to measure the benefit of this revenue expenditure.

To return to the DMA definition given above, FM is achieved through:

> ... the provision of highly trained and skilfully managed staff to conduct brand-building activities on behalf of a client. These staff all work for the FM company, to which the client has outsourced a marketing activity to meet specific goals and targets. The staff used will interact, explain, shock, assist or pacify and, above all, give feedback to the client while developing the client's brand in line with the brand strategies, and nurturing the brand with CRM that is specific, targeted and measurable.

The need for the highest standards of ethical operation apply to FM. Significant work in the people sector over the last 15 years has seen the development of people skills, and the higher standards of work now implemented in the field have thrown off the old premise that FM employs out-of-work actors. Given that the quality of staffing is available, and it is, the industry is now providing proper remuneration and management structure. However, this is not universal, and the industry is damaged by the agencies seeking to cut costs and conducting work solely on low prices. This is one sector where you get what you pay for.

In summary, FM is a very effective brand builder that is a highly accountable brand communication, which uses fantastic people to deliver a sales and marketing strategy.

The FM disciplines

The FMC acknowledges six disciplines within FM. These are each described fully in their own chapter. A brief overview follows:

- Sales. This FM discipline includes: strategic sales, tactical sales, a sales campaign. This is where a highly targeted, trained FM team is brought in either over a long period of time or for a one-off action to stimulate sales of a brand, and gains distribution and sales.
- Merchandising. This is a very important part of brand awareness, ensuring good product placement or service presence and correct pricing as well as product availability in sufficient quantity to meet demand, giving brand visibility and presence.
- Auditing. This includes recording information on a brand to establish its presence, availability, distribution and position in a market place. Analysis can then be conducted that will show a way forward to improve the results, or maintain them if they are positive.
- Sampling and demonstrating. Sampling is when the consumer is offered the opportunity to try, usually by tasting or smelling a product. Demonstrating is when the product or service is shown or demonstrated to consumers: the consumer observes but does not always operate the product as demonstrated.
- Experiential marketing, road shows, events. Experiential marketing is live and interactive marketing that builds positive emotional sensory engagement between a brand and its consumers. A road show is when a promotional activity is created, which then moves from location to location. An event is a promotional activity that does not move!
- Mystery calling and shopping. These are covert face-to-face approaches in which a trained mystery shopper will visit an outlet to make assessments.

Industry size

The value of FM to the Direct Marketing industry rose 5 per cent in 2005 to an estimated value of £ 770 million. (DMA Census, 2005). The 2006 numbers will only be available in 2007 after this book has gone to print.

Who uses FM?

Key sectors for FM

The sectors in which FM operates are diverse as shown by the chart below (source: FMC, 2003). There has been no research done since 2003 to evidence the current users, and further research is not expected until late in 2007. Very loosely speaking, if the chart shown below were updated there

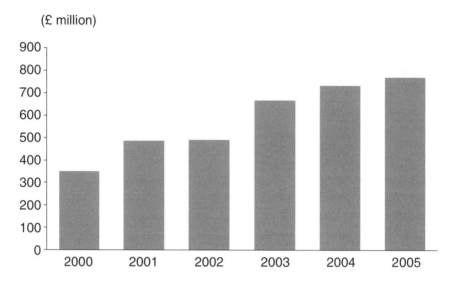

(£ million)

Source: DMA Census of the Direct Marketing Industry, 2005

Figure 0.1 UK field marketing annual turnover

would probably not be much of a shift, although the level of utilities would be lower than the 4.4 per cent shown.

The profile of FM users

- Companies wanting professional customer relationships, and engaging consumer relationships that will push and drive their brands towards success and profits, must look to FM as a part of their strategy to achieve these goals.
- Anyone who believes that marketing is about the bottom line **before** it is about interior design.
- Anyone with a sales and marketing budget who wants to see his or her product or service develop as a brand more specifically by being:
  - in front of the prospective purchaser, correctly placed, in prime position, with sufficient facings;
  - distributed across the entire marketplace, including multiples, independents and specialists;
  - displayed in the proper manner: at the correct price, with correct POS accompaniment, in the proper section of the store or office;

Proportion of field marketing expenditure by sector

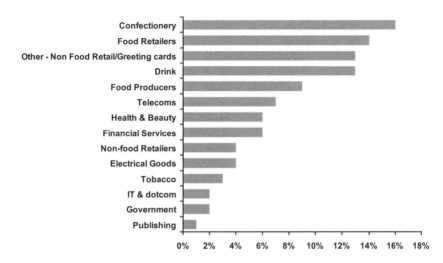

Source: DMA Field Marketing Council. DMA Research Centre, 2005

Figure 0.2 Key sectors for FM

- – understood by the retailers so that they can effectively communicate the brand's features, benefits and values;
- – part of a regular ordering and stocking procedure so the brand is never out of stock;
- – monitored on a daily, weekly or monthly basis in the field using real-time reporting, so that irregularities are spotted and sales opportunities maximized.

Having achieved the above, the discerning FM user may then want to improve sales further by:

- ● developing brand awareness with the consumer or end user;
- ● generating an understanding of brand values;
- ● allowing the product to be sampled or trialled so as to involve and educate the end user;
- ● selling the product or service to end users using direct sales;
- ● supporting the outlets selling the brand to sell it well, with training and incentives to improve sales further;
- ● responding to market changes by 'tweaking' the activities to meet the changes, even as the activity is running.

All of these objectives can be achieved by FM.

Having delivered all the above and more the FM user will then have the benefit of being able to know how much the activity has delivered to the bottom line, so that effective spend can be defined.

The final benefit to the FM user is to be released from the day-to-day commitment of running people, training, employment, applying best practice, planning, and yet benefit from all the advantages detailed above. If you would like to achieve all the above in your business, then you need FM. The same applies to the non-retailer too, including charities, professional bodies and the public sector (see below). In the non-retail sectors the problem is simply one of a need for awareness of FM. Just think of the improved response and take-up of course places, training, etc to a highly targeted sales campaign including placing the right material in front of potential delegates or members.

Types of FM projects or campaigns

As in other disciplines, there are different types of campaigns that can be applied to any FM discipline:

- A short-term campaign (also called a tactical campaign in the FM industry) is one that operates within a finite time span, for example a two-week audit, a three-month sales drive. This will meet a short-term need without disrupting a company, in a comparatively condensed time frame. The focus is on either message delivery to the consumers by involving, exciting and educating them, or to a retailer by introducing ideas or products to him or her or developing a specific campaign.
- An ongoing campaign (also called a strategic campaign in the FM industry) is ongoing on a full-time basis, and is designed to reach a large marketing target. These campaigns focus on the delivery of brand strategy, and the usual length of contract is two to three years.
- Consistent ongoing campaign activity is a campaign that is not full time. This third type of work falls between the other two, and is conducted for a long period of time, say a year or more, but it does not offer full-time work. It might for example occupy two days a month for a one-year period. Again there is a focus on delivering brand strategy.

The legal pitfalls

This book gives guidance in the complex areas of employment law, health and safety, legal and proper placement of the activity and the rules regarding the set-up, operation and closure of an activity. These are very many and very varied, for example a penalty may be imposed by a local council for unlicensed handouts of free literature accompanying an FM event. See Chapter 17 regarding these issues.

Suffice it to say that the rules and regulations are often complex and ever changing, so be sure that you are comfortable that the FM company you recruit has the ability to deal with all these issues.

How to use this book

Scope of the book

The purpose of the book is to give readers the confidence and understanding to make decisions about the FM activities that they should include in their integrated marketing plan (to achieve their marketing objectives). The book will also provide the knowledge, skill and understanding to enable readers to understand something of the implementation of FM activities, so that they can more fully understand their FM agency and work with them more easily.

Structure of the book

There are two parts to this book: Part 1 deals with the context and the principles of FM and Part 2 with practical techniques. They are designed to be read and used differently.

Part 1 has 11 chapters, which can be summarized as follows:

- Chapter 1 starts with the customer. It considers customers and how they reach the decision point at which to buy, how they are affected by branding, and the importance of influencers. It goes on the consider the resulting sales process and integrated marketing solutions that match the customer need with the presentation and promotion of the offer and how a brand is important.
- Chapter 2 deals with the business and marketing purpose behind FM – how FM fits into a business or organization's activities and the business process that determines their extent and use.
- Chapter 3 explains what FM can do – the objectives that FM can achieve.
- Chapters 4 to 9 deal with each of the FM disciplines in the FM toolbox in more detail. For each of the FM activities above the book describes:

- the marketing activity on its own: what it is and what it can and cannot achieve, how to control the activity, how to measure the success of the activity;
- its role as a marketing activity as part of an integrated marketing approach within the marketing communications mix;
- possible measures of achievement, accountability, setting a key performance indicator (KPI) and how such achievement is measured;
- the practical use, tips and the specific implementation of each of the FM activities and the added value that FM will bring to the exercise and the brand.
- Chapters 10 and 11 describe all the ancillaries that you need to have in place to carry out FM. Essential reading!

Part 2 has eight chapters that cover FM practice:

- Chapter 12 describes when to use the FM disciplines, how and in what combinations.
- Chapter 13 describes how FM operations are carried out by FM agencies to avoid disaster and ensure that all the elements work together. FM operations stand or fall on the details of their implementation.
- Chapter 14, on accountability and ROI, is essential for ensuring that your field promotions meet the FM and marketing objectives you set.
- Chapter 15 looks at briefing, choosing and procuring FM agencies.
- Chapter 16 examines how to maximize the return on your investment in FM and the role of creativity and innovation in FM – introducing an element of fun for customers. The chapter adds tips that come from decades of experience and is essential reading.
- Chapter 17 covers the legal aspects of FM, including employment law, staff pay, insurance and health and safety. FM involves a lot of people working in many different environments, so to be legal and correct FM practitioners have to be well versed in these areas. It is also a fact that any promotional activity must be legal, and while this most usually applies to sales promotion and advertising, agencies must check the legality of promotions. Advice is given in this chapter.
- Chapter 18 covers international FM, in theory and in practice.
- Chapter 19 covers, for completeness, the in-house face-to-face scene.

A set of self-study questions is at the end of each chapter to help you make the most of this book. The questions are for the student specifically but also readers wishing to see if they have grasped the chapter's lessons. The questions have been devised to see that basic concepts have been absorbed. The answers are given in the text of the chapter.

If you are tempted to dive straight into the practice techniques and skip Part 1, resist. You can use the practical techniques to best effect only if you are clear about the why, when and how of FM. You will find Part 2 useful for years to come. You may not want to read it all at once. You will probably want to dip into it and refer to it for the nuts and bolts of practical techniques that you may want to use now or in the future. If you are studying for a marketing course, you will find the data you need on the range of techniques available to you.

At the end of the book there is a chapter of further information, listing useful addresses, books, magazines and courses and a short glossary. The organizations listed have a descriptive sentence to explain how they can best help you. Some organizations compiled their entry themselves. FM has developed a jargon over the years that would frustrate the academic. In the book the authors have used both the FM industry jargon (used by clients and agencies) and explained the meanings alongside in generally accepted practitioner terms. This particularly applies to Chapter 14.

There are case studies throughout the book, illustrating the best in FM practice. Use these for ideas for your business sector and your business challenge. They have been placed in the chapter to which they mainly refer. They illustrate FM disciplines and their use in different business sectors as well. The problem with including case studies is that they inevitably become out of date. Please refer to the DMA website at www.dma.org.uk which, in addition to including examples of FM in its 2005 and 2006 awards section, has links to members' websites. The authors found difficulty in sourcing case studies. The FM industry purpose is considered a well-kept secret and some FM agencies consider their clients would not like disclosure.

What is not in this book

Anything that is not face-to-face marketing is not covered in this book. This includes all indirect promotions such as advertising, public relations and all direct marketing other than face-to-face and sales promotions (so the following are not FM: selling by direct mail, door to door, catalogues, mail order, leaflets, handouts, direct response TV, e-mails, telemarketing – other than telephone calls used as a part of FM disciplines to make best use of budgets).

See the 'Further information' section for the contact details of useful organizations and 'References and further reading' for additional texts.

Part 1

Principles

1 Starting with the customer

Customers and their behaviour

Why do you need to start with the customer?

At the heart of every successful business is a close understanding of customers' needs and how to anticipate and meet them. For many years, people understood this unconsciously, long before 'marketing' was invented; it was the genius of every great entrepreneur.

When not many alternatives were produced and there was relatively little choice, customers took what they were offered; it was the day of the salesperson. But those days passed. In an interim period it was thought to be part of the task of a marketing department to make customers aware of the benefits and then for sales to persuade and sell. Now customers have an amazing amount of choice, they generally serve and select the products themselves and the task is to convince them, to really want to buy from (directly, or from others indirectly,) your brand – again and again. A brand can now be marketed and promoted such that it becomes bonded to the customer. Tesco has achieved this. A tribe follows Richard Branson's Virgin brand.

The age of no salesperson involvement seems to be passing and people do expect a relationship with a brand and for the brand to be delivered so that they can experience it, so that it reinforces their perception and belief in the brand. They also expect to see a brand to which they are bonded, in place, in their preferred outlets, in quantities such that it is always available. It is a part of their comfort zone and confidence in their preferred brands. If the brand they prefer is not there, then anger may arise and a competitor brand will perhaps be selected. Customers then make a further decision as to whether to buy then and there, or to pursue the cheapest offer, for example via the internet.

When a need or a problem arises for the customer the onus was once on the customer to initiate the dialogue and make contact. Now people in firms are going back to seeing customers' needs as everyone's concern, not just the concern of a marketing department. Increasingly, firms are sharing responsibility for thinking about customer needs among line managers in every functional discipline. It is not that marketing has gone out of fashion, it is that the customer has come of age and demands attention from all parts of the firm. Marketing has been generalized across the firm as a whole – and rightly so – and in every situation when the customer contacts your brand. This means in all outlets where your brand is expected to be sold, even if a representative of your firm is not there. This has a great impact on the operational side of retail. Placement in the store, and appropriate stock level and shelf filling must match the customer expectation. The supplier pays for and equally expects a standard of service to support the brand at the POS. This is where FM comes in. It delivers the brand promise to the customer at the POS. The key is the delivery mechanism – the FM person – with whom the customer develops the relationship, who creates for the customer the brand awareness and offers brand experience; the person who brings the brand alive – the brand ambassador.

And do not think the above just applies to retail. The retail customer may also be a B2B buyer (for an organization, for themselves as a small business or as a self-employed person), or a member of a professional body, (they are certainly a member of the public) and the same approach is expected. Delivery of product or service is expected to meet the brand's standards – and comparisons are made with other competitors' brands.

Identifying your customer

Remember that customers are affected by their background, and their social or cultural influences; they consider and think of matters in different ways; they have varied economic purchasing power, they have different levels of intelligence; and they have prejudices. Clearly you need to understand your existing and potential customers – whoever they are. You need to find out all about them to serve them better, retain their custom and persuade them to buy more. Everyone in your organization needs to know about them. Equally the customer will be finding out about your company as epitomized by your brand as a supplier; it is a two-way communication. In finding out about each other, you will establish a relationship. Making sure you do that well and that the customer trusts your firm and your brand, is called customer relationship management (CRM). You should aim to provide a consistent customer experience wherever and whenever the customer touches the brand.

Identify your customer and establish a customer profile – an idealized, averaged, but complete understanding of the way the customers think; what influences them; how, when, what and from whom they are prepared to buy. It is really important to grasp this. If you understand the customers, you have a chance of persuading them to buy. If you do not understand them you are less likely to be able to persuade them to buy. Without customers you make no sales; with no sales, a business dies.

Marketing is tasked with identifying and knowing the customer. If you discover that there is more than one common type of customer, each with a different approach to buying from you, then you have segments. Each of the different, yet identifiable, separate customer groups is known as a segment. Sorting all types of customers by segments is called market segmentation. Market segmentation is only helpful where each segment has a different approach to buying, and is of a size and has the purchasing power, accessibility and future viability from which you will make a profit.

If you are selling to buyers and the buyers are selling on your product or service to customers who are consumers, marketing will need to understand both tiers of customers – that is, the primary buyers and the primary buyers' own buyers, who could be consumers. If you are dealing with B2B customers, their customers may also be business customers. There are differences within each tier. You need to know and understand them all.

FM recognizes the importance of matching people in face-to-face situations to the customers. Databases allow the characteristics of salespersons to be stored, so that when there is a requirement to match a particular target audience with appropriate FM personnel, the right skills are found.

Think from the customer's viewpoint

People carry baggage from the culture and social environment of their upbringing, their education and their life experience, and it is easy to make assumptions about how others think and are likely to respond to communications with them. Accept the fact that the people you are selling to are unlikely to have the same background as yourself. If you don't, you may have a problem grasping the need for marketing. It is easy to assume that one target group of customers is a segment much like another, to ignore research highlighting differences, and to apply what you have done before – because it's easy, because it may have worked before, because... Everyone has convincing reasons for doing what they have always done and forgetting the research. Don't ignore you market research: believe it and act on it.

Before you go any further, for every customer segment that you decide to select as a target (you do not need to target every one), you should apply the following method. Erase from your mind your own thinking and prejudices. Learn to listen, observe and grasp how your target thinks, communicates and comes to conclusions. You need to understand what makes the target tick, react, etc. This method has been described as 'self-recognition criteria' – accepting that the way you think and react is certainly wrong for any target you are analysing. You should not make any assumptions about the target customer. Find out.

Now that we have an open mind about the customers, let's find out what makes them tick and how they express their needs.

The new customer on the block

Marketing Week (Parker, 2006) suggests in 2007 a further new step: you need to identify the future shapers among your customers and engage with them. Future shapers are identified as:

- valuing authenticity and originality in all they buy and experience;
- well informed and hugely involved in products, services and brands they buy;
- individualistic; doing things their way and try to persuade suppliers to convert to that way;
- time poor, valuing anything that saves them time;
- socially responsible, exercising ethical awareness via product and brand choices;
- curious, open-minded and receptive to new ideas;
- advocates of new ideas – and they spread the word.

The new marketing mix – the offer – the six Cs

Matching the customers' expectations

The offer is the supplier's answer to the customers' needs meeting the customers' expectation. Customers' needs, in any particular area, are met by product or service offerings alongside a bundle of characteristics – the six Cs: cost, convenience, concept, communication, customer relationship and consistency, known together as the offer (see the table on the next pages for a full description). Some Cs the organization controls entirely, and some not. The offer is described in the language of your customers, using their perceptions. It is the new marketing mix for now and the future; this is what an organization has to consider when it is thinking of what to promote, and what to sell to the customer – and from the customer's perspective.

The old way of describing the marketing mix was the four Ps (see below); now just think of the six Cs. (The six Cs were developed by Roddy Mullin and Cathy Ace separately in 2001). The Cs are referred to by Kotler (a guru of marketing) in 2005 as offering a better view of the marketing mix as it is from the buyer's perspective.

The offer

- Cost. A customer considers cost (and cost of ownership) within a value perception. That value perception is personal and includes a quality of life assessment. This is often based on brands with which the person wishes to be associated. A customer also puts into the equation the cost of time and travel to make a purchase. The Future Foundation research indicates that consumers will travel for most of their activities and purchases within a 14-mile radius of their home.
- Convenience of buying. This includes a mix of location, opening hours, cash, cheque or credit card acceptability. Customers are lazy – exercising the brain requires effort and energy – so make it easy for them, and convenient for them to buy.
- Concept. This is a mix of product and service. The whole concept (the product and service together) you are offering as a supplier must match what customers need, want and perceive to be the solution to their need, offering greater benefit – ie an advantage – over other suppliers. It has to be provided at a cost, and in a manner

that the customers want. Few products are sold without some sort of aftercare service. The quality and fitness for purpose of the concept are assumed to be right. A warranty or return policy is taken for granted. A brand is principally a consolidation of the concept (although the other Cs come into it) into an easy-to-remember space in the mind of the customer.

- Communication. Consider how well the product or service is communicated to the customer. This is where FM really comes into its own, matching communicating with the feel of the brand at the POS. Customers will not buy if communication is too complex, too dull or does not put the concept across in terms they commonly use. FM is the perfect answer, as the FM personnel can listen, answer queries, respond, empathize, and relate to the customer. No other marketing discipline does that on the spot with the customer. FM can report back to clients the comments, feelings, and misunderstandings that a consumer may have about a brand, and indeed include the nuances of the consumer's emotions. The mobile internet is the consumer technology of the future – certainly in the UK where 86 per cent of the population own at least one (96 per cent of 16–34-year-olds, 58 per cent of the over 65s). It is always switched on. It is always with the consumer. And the consumer is developing relationships with their preferred brands. They look at the websites and register to receive e-mails. Alerts to brand experience (FM) opportunities will be the key – as has been achieved with the young – with viral marketing text messaging in the drinks trade in the last few years. Mobile advertising may possibly take off as the mobile internet incorporates TV as well. Communicating through mobiles accounts for 16 per cent of communication with radio audiences.

- Customer relationship. CRM principles apply. Customers expect to be treated with respect at all times and that all reasonable questions will be answered and problems resolved. Once they have made a purchase of any size or have signed up for a service, they expect to be recognized and remembered. For example, once a customer has had a car serviced at a garage, he or she expects the garage to know all the car's idiosyncrasies when he or she calls. People like to build relationships; you have to accept this. If customers get different answers from different people or departments in the same organization, they tend to trust the people and the organization less. 'Integration' means making sure every part of your business delivers consistent answers. Research shows an integrated approach is worth 30 per cent of sales (or a loss of 30 per cent if you do not practise it). FM delivers customer relationships in spades! Face-to-face selling – you cannot do better than that.

- Consistency. This is the reassurance of ongoing quality and reliability of the other five Cs – brand surety if you like. It is integration and comes from applying internal marketing within an organization – all aware of the brand values.

Source: Mullin, 2001

It's all in the mind of the customer

Branding

This is the process of lodging your offer in the customers' mind to remind them you exist just as and when they need you. The 'shorthand' mind retention device is your logo or brand name. If you have it right, the shorthand encompasses the six Cs – the offer above. It is a powerful thing, a successful brand and when you achieve brand bonding the world is your oyster; or rather, you will sell more. Remember the reminding bit: this means you will need to market your brand to customers regularly.

Buying process and behaviour

This involves understanding that customers adopt a buying process, different for different purchases, which they have developed in their mind as an appropriate way to purchase products and services. You have the task of finding out what it is and developing a sales process to match. Research shows that many first generation internet sites forgot the need to match the way their customers buy. A number of models describe how people buy: one is the involvement model.

The involvement model for buying is increasingly being seen as a more realistic description of the way in which consumers buy products and services. The model extends well beyond marketing. The Church, for example, used to think that people started belonging to a church because they believed – often after a conversion experience. However, it is now understood that people belong before they believe. Studies have shown that people become involved in a church because of friends or family. It is often quite casual at first. Only after a period of years do they come to realize that they believe. The process of 'belonging before believing' is about 'behaviour before attitude'.

FM is, first and foremost, about behaviour. It offers the chance to experience a product and the brand values that come with it. Once you have seen that the product or service matches or could match your preferred behaviour then if the process continues, it is only a question of time before the attitude follows the behaviour. It makes increasing sense in the light of evidence that behaviour precedes attitude. Encouraging someone to try a product or service is often the best way to begin the process by which they become a long-term customer and develop a relationship with your brand and your firm.

Behaviour and attitude have a complicated relationship with each other. Practical examples illustrate this. Surveys show that far more people think that regular exercise is a good thing (attitude) than actually practise it (behaviour). Surveys also show that people drink more alcohol (behaviour) than they are prepared to admit (attitude). For years, the government urged people to use seat belts (attitude) with only limited effect. They then passed a law making it a crime not to wear them (behaviour). People grumbled at first, but buckled up. Over time, their attitude changed to accord with the behaviour they had become accustomed to. This suggests that marketing campaigns that directly impact on the behaviour of customers succeed, and the desired attitude to the product or service will follow. FM does this. Advertising campaigns aimed primarily at creating awareness and changing attitudes are less likely to succeed.

The role of influencers

Customers are influenced by others when making purchases and this influence must be understood. You need to know how those around the customers, the people they follow and their perceived status, can influence their attitude and their buying behaviour. You should use people to whom the customer can relate to sell, to demonstrate and to join with the customer as they experience the product or service and learn about the brand.

This book considers the customer viewpoint hereafter in terms of the six Cs, accepting branding as shorthand, recognizing that a buying process exists and that behaviour must be studied, and noting the part influencers play.

Managing the brand – influencing the mind of the customer

The bundle of characteristics – the six Cs – the new marketing mix, is your offer, the brand promise. Truly great brands achieve leadership in all dimensions, having superlative quality, unbeatable value and outstanding image in the six Cs offered. Making the most of 'brand equity' – the sum of quality, value and image as customers understand it – is one of the crucial jobs for any manager. As more businesses realize that a company is its brand, so more CEOs and MDs manage the brand. Evidence exists that customers ultimately bond with a brand, not bothering to look elsewhere, as long as that brand delivers the brand promise. Bonding exceeds any loyalty. It has become a CEO deliverable. It gives a value far in excess of the bricks and mortar worth of a company.

The most difficult element of a brand for any firm to manage is the psychological part; that is achieving and retaining ownership of a piece of the customers' mind. Companies often talk about creating an image. They may do so in the minds of the staff who work long and hard to devise it. They only do so in customers' minds when customers adapt, develop and absorb that image as their own. Companies can offer an image, but they cannot make an image. If it is attractive and powerful, and accords with customers' own experiences, it will form part of their image of the product or service. Thoughts and images in our own minds are, thankfully, beyond anyone else's total control.

Customers retain perceptions and images, and their own key senses trigger a brand if the retention has been successful. It is a shorthand memory device, a mix of logo, and slogan or a feeling that the customer relates to advantage with regard to a need. If you have such recall in a customer, you are made. But beware: if the concept you are selling does not match the perception, image and experience of the customer, you are far less likely to make a sale. You also need to nurture that retention constantly and favourably reinforce it. FM does this well at the POS.

It is quite possible to have different perceptions of your brand in different parts of the globe or even in different parts of one country. Guinness for a time advertised in Africa, unwittingly using a symbol that communicated that Guinness improved fertility. Brylcreem was thought to be a food delicacy in another African country. A failure of branding you might think – unless of course you are happy to sell with that branding mismatch.

It is also quite possible to reposition a brand. Sometimes this is essential to save a brand that has become dusty and is failing. Failures are often the seed corn of success if the lesson is understood. Lucozade was rebranded as a sports drink from its previous life as an expensive drink for when you were ill. It used to be said that you knew you were really ill when the Lucozade appeared. How different it is now.

The four Ps (the old marketing mix) and why they are no longer relevant

Just in case you are asked about the old four Ps marketing mix, read these paragraphs. There was a time when business was thought of as a series of functions all capable of operating in isolation. Marketing was a function; sales was a function; production was a function. These functions operated in silos.

Organizationally based marketing traditionally considers the needs of the customer in terms of four Ps: the product or service, the place, the price, the promotion. (Note: others added Ps for process, people and physical evidence to make it seven Ps. Kotler once added politics.) This approach gives the wrong perspective for the marketing needs analysis of the customer in the 21st century and the subsequent decision making about which marketing activities to apply. It is better to approach the needs of the customers (whether buyers or consumers) *in terms of their view* of the four Ps. What you are really doing is applying self-recognition criteria – looking at the Ps – from the customers' view. And when you do this, the four Ps become six Cs.

Separate functions, such as finance, production and marketing, continue to exist in firms, and they can be managed well or badly. A good marketing department, however, does not create a competitive advantage on its own any longer. Its work is part of a process that takes place every time someone buys or uses the company's products or services. It is part of the process by which relationships are strengthened, and by which customer and other stakeholder needs are satisfied. Think of it as part of the creation and strengthening of relationships that contribute to the success of the business. The leading management thinker John Kay writes: 'I see the firm as a set of relationships between its various stakeholders – employees, customers, investors and shareholders. The successful firm is one which creates a distinctive character in these relationships and which operates in an environment that maximizes the value of that distinctiveness.

What characterizes these relationships? Money plays a large part, whether in salaries for staff, dividends to shareholders or invoices to customers. However, there is much more to it than that – like loyalty, expectation and human feeling. Whether people buy a product or work for a firm, they are engaged in a relationship that satisfies their needs to a greater or lesser extent. The task of business is to maximize the value of that relationship. The four Ps approach matched a business structure where relationships did not feature and only hierarchical silos existed.

FM and ethics

As this chapter deals with the customer, it is right that the duty of care to the customer is covered here.

There is always a temptation in FM, as in many other areas of business, to cut corners, to promise more than you intend to give, and to rely on the small print as a get-out. Is this good business if you can get away with it? Some people think so, but they are a declining minority. The reason is that relationships are increasingly seen as central to business success. It is unwise to treat badly those with whom you want to build up a long-term relationship.

In 1995 the Royal Society of Arts published a report entitled *Tomorrow's Company*, with backing from some of Britain's top business leaders. This argued that successful companies are those that have a 'success model' that embraces the interests of all their stakeholders – shareholders, customers, suppliers, employees and community (RSA, 1995). A study of the United States' most visionary companies in 1996 found that those businesses that were consistently most successful were the ones that did not place profit first, but in second place to a core ideology that often stressed responsibility to others.

Across the world, there is evidence that people prefer to deal with companies they trust. 'The company behind the brand' is increasingly important. Richard Branson's rating as the UK's most admired business leader has helped Virgin diversify from records to air travel to personal finance and drinks.

An ethic of enlightened self-interest guides companies not to abuse customer relationships by subjecting people to sharp FM practice. However, FM practitioners have another and more specific ethical challenge to consider: if FM is effective in changing behaviour, it is a powerful and double-edged weapon that can change behaviour for the bad as well as the good.

FM in the UK is largely guided by internal self-regulation, policed by the industry via the DMA. The FMC works hard to ensure that the self-regulation works, and is enforced and effective. It has codes and publishes guidelines of best practice. Members are inspected to ensure they comply, and an accreditation scheme exists for which consultation, input and endorsement is being sought by such bodies as CIPS (Chartered Institute of Procurement and Supplies). In most of Europe, there are greater legislative rather than self-regulation controls.

Summary

In the 21st century the customer is really aware of marketing and all its facets. The offer presented by the marketer must meet the needs of the customer in terms of the six Cs, match customers' preferred buying process and fulfil the brand promise.

In the absence of human contact at the decision point – the point of selecting the item to buy – the choice of competing products is daunting. It is then that FM comes into its own. There, just as the customers expected, is the brand they prefer, just waiting to be bought, with the brand ambassador – the FM person – in close attendance to create awareness, demonstrate, allow experience and communicate the brand values.

Self-study questions

1.1. To ensure that you have understood, write a short sentence on each of the six Cs – the offer – describing what needs of the customer each C covers. Then, as an exercise, write down the six Cs of your own business or organization's offer.
1.2. Based on your organization's offer prepare a brand values statement – what would you want your customers to hold in their mind?
1.3. Describe the difference between attitude and behaviour; which is more important to the marketer in the long term, which in the short term?
1.4. Why is understanding the customer first so important in business?

(Answers can be found in the text.)

2 The business and marketing purpose behind FM

Introduction to the business process

How do business and marketing fit together and how does FM fit into that? Take an example. A business vision may be to 'grow the business', that is to sell more; one of the related business objectives for the year ahead specifies a target sales figure. The business meets the target. Wonderful. The objective is met and a part of the vision achieved.

Business objectives come from your business vision or mission, or the tasks you see that lie ahead and are usually related to a time period – often a year, sometimes two years ahead. Marketing helps provide some of the strategic inputs to help decide those business objectives. If, for example, market research discovers it is likely that the market is going to cease then you may decide not to pursue that particular business objective. It is similar to entering a film-based camera business as the market goes digital.

Following is a figure that illustrates how marketing interfaces with a business and the customer. It shows the part market intelligence plays in deciding whether to proceed with the business venture, confirming that you can sell sufficient of your product or service to make money at the price the customer is prepared to pay, and that there are sufficient potential customers and that you can afford to operate from a customer's preferred locations. (Let's assume you can make money; if not stop! The authors' experience sadly finds this is not always the case.) This strategic exercise has to be repeated from time to time. A business dies if it does not review the market and change to match. Think of the changes many businesses have had to make as the customer went from horses to cars; from smoking to non-smoking, from video to DVD.

Figure 2.1 shows that from certain business objectives, through derived marketing objectives and after considering the alternative solutions, one set of options is selected and a marketing plan is formed. The marketing plan sets out the marketing activities (and a group of marketing activities towards one marketing objective may be called a campaign) that are to be undertaken to persuade the customers to change their behaviour and attitude favourably towards a supplier, accepting the business' offer. This includes receiving the brand experience and brand values and at the point of purchase (POP) (sales) matching with a sales process, the customers' preferred way to buy.

How marketing fits into a business

The figure also shows other marketing activities. Marketing promotion includes advertising, PR and non face-to-face direct marketing and sales pro-

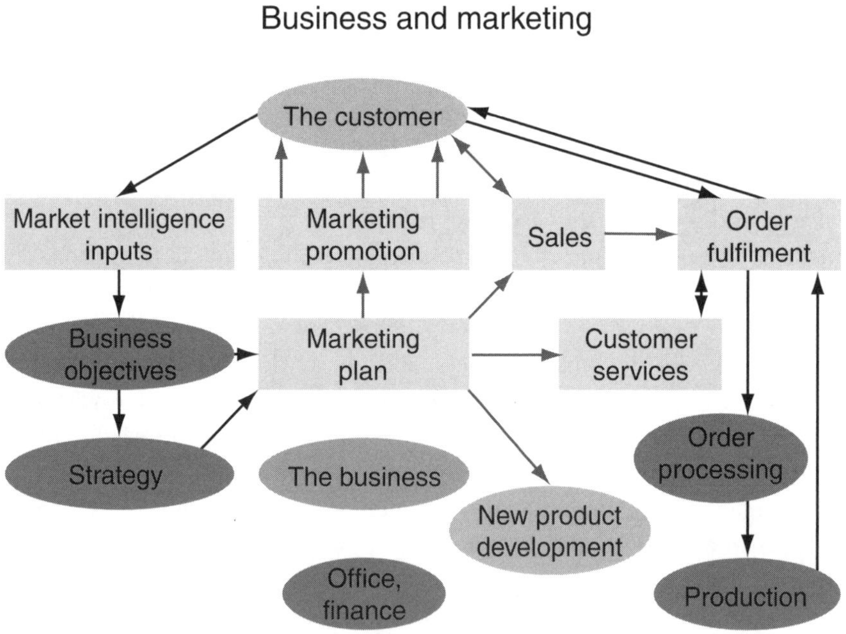

Business and marketing

Figure 2.1 How marketing fits into a business
Source: Mullin (2006)

motion. Sales is face-to-face with the customer at the POP (this is the part that includes FM) and once the sale is made, there is an order fulfilment process where customer services people deal with any customer difficulties. Order fulfilment itself may be the service provider for a service product, for example with hairdressers or garages which are principally offering a service. Marketing also becomes involved with new product (or service) development. Some parts of the business may not interact with the customer directly – towards completion the figure illustrates this with the office and finance element. Finance may become involved with the customer on credit assessment and poor payments, although this is usually handled through customer services. The diagram is illustrative to show the marketing parts of the business. Note that marketing is the key interface at every point with the customer.

Having seen illustrated simply how marketing operates within a business, now consider what marketing in its various parts can do, describing each as a marketing tool. The tools are shown in Figure 2.2 and follow a logical sequence – the order in which they are applied. The diagram shows all the marketing tools and the sequence by tool number that should follow the market research. FM is the face-to-face part of direct marketing, itself a part of promotion.

The market research tool finds out customers' needs, competitors' activity and 'whole market' intelligence. Market research is essential to establish your position in the minds of customers and how they rate your products and services. There are market research specialists operating individually, as agencies or huge global organizations such as Taylor Nelson Soffres (TNS). Whom you use for market research, and how often, may be budget dependent but you should do some and it should be unbiased – that is you should use someone unconnected with your business and who understands how to do it – a chartered marketer.

From market research you can then define the offer and the brand values (these marketing tools are described in Chapter 1). Then you need to promote both your offer and your brand values helping you to decide which to go for. Market research should have found the customer preferences for media, channels and formats. You may add an appropriate sales promotion if it adds zip or fun and your potential customers appreciate them. You will also be able to establish a sales process.

FM as a relative newcomer to the marketing canvas is often not considered as one of the marketing activities to meet a marketing objective. Reading this book may be the first time many businesses will meet, learn and understand just what it can do and how powerful it is. In part their ignorance is due to a wish by those who do use FM not to let competitors know about it. There are FM agencies and their clients who do not allow their campaigns to be

MARKETING TOOLS

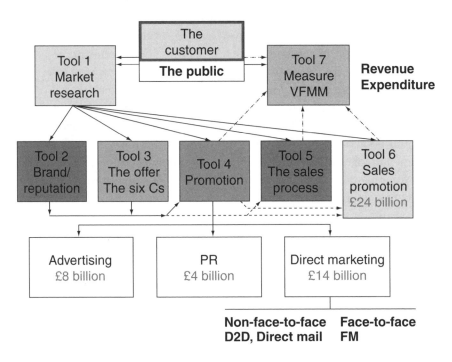

Figure 2.2 Marketing tools for the marketer
Source: Mullin (2006); figures from ISP

showcased as the detail and the results could lose them their marketing edge, if their competitors picked up on it.

FM – the face-to-face part of the promotion

The FM objective within a marketing objective is much narrower in focus. It is concerned with ensuring that customers, having bought in to your brand, can then buy the products and services at their local retail outlet with whom you have negotiated prime shelf space. The buy in to your brand may also be an FM activity – you set up a sampling and display event in a series of a multiples' car parks to increase brand awareness and allow brand experience. The FM objective derives from the business objective you have set and the marketing objectives that followed. It is specifically related to the POS (Chapters 4 to 9 cover each of the FM disciplines and Chapter 3 gives an overview).

Objectives we choose in our personal lives work in a similar way. You may be reading this book because you want to advance your career in business or marketing. Learning about FM follows from that, but it is not the only way you could advance your career. Once you have decided you want to learn about FM, you rightly focus on the best means of achieving it – of which reading this book is one. Similarly you need to consider whether FM is the best way to achieve a marketing objective. It depends on your offer and the brand values you wish to put across.

The next chapter identifies objectives that are most commonly addressed by FM, the disciplines available and how to put them together to achieve the behavioural change that you want. Following this process will not guarantee that your FM will be a world beater. However, it will ensure that it is fit for the task and that it logically connects with business and marketing objectives.

Business and marketing objectives

This book is not about how to write business plans or marketing plans but to explain how FM activities complete the picture and how they can be used as part of your promotional mix – the face-to-face part – in an integrated fashion to deliver the marketing mix (the offer) you have drawn up.

Companies sometimes fail to identify that there actually are business tasks to be done. Business tasks come in a variety of forms. They can be: moving offices, setting up a new production line, helping accounts with new software, etc. Thinking clearly about your business and where you want it to be in this coming year and in the future as part of that is not difficult. It is a useful mind-clearing process. The paragraphs that follow are purely to illustrate the business process and show how FM disciplines should be selected and how they end up as part of the marketing plan. First it is important to convert the business tasks to business objectives.

Business and marketing objectives must be SMART: specific, measurable, agreed, reasonable and timebound. Check each objective, whether it is a business, marketing or promotional objective, as you write it to see that it meets each of the SMART criteria.

Illustrative business objectives

It is useful here to look at an example. Suppose you are a director of a small sports equipment business. You sell to outlets that sell to consumers. You have business tasks that are to grow the business, modernize, update, relocate and introduce FM which you have heard is amazing in the way it increases business. Finally, you want to have a better position in the sports sector than your nearest competitor – this is apparently another key outcome of using FM. The SMART business objectives, in order of priority, for a company doing business in sports or leisure might be as follows:

- To sell the existing range of products, with the revamped basic product, to achieve the increased target sales (a figure in £s is included here) within the calendar year. (This objective effectively defines the market share your firm is going for.)
- To move the headquarters offices and three regional sales offices to new premises in the summer layoff. (There are no marketing implications here, but plenty of indirect implications!)
- To grow the customer base by 10 per cent, that is 40 new long-term customers (ie outlets through which to sell your products) by the end of the year.
- To introduce FM in the next six months.
- To achieve a profile at the end of the year that places the perception and image, ie brand, of this firm and its products above those of your direct competitor (with a list of attributes, benefits and features to be agreed by the end of January).
- To upgrade the machinery in the B production shop to retain labour costs while increasing production by 10 per cent. (There will be no marketing impact unless the new machinery is delayed in introduction and there is no product to sell.)
- To take a stand at the main relevant sport exhibition.
- To raise the awareness to 80 per cent by the end of the year, among those that play, watch or train in the sport, of the purpose of your business and the concept – products and/or services – it provides.

Not all the business objectives affect marketing. But from these business objectives you can then draw up marketing objectives, which might be:

- To achieve the sales targets set (figure in £s) including sales of one relaunched product in the year ahead.
- To increase consumer and customer awareness and understanding of the products and their purpose so that unprompted recall is higher than for your competitor's products at the end of the year.
- To relaunch the product at the main exhibition.
- To introduce and use FM disciplines within six months.

- To grow the customer database by 10 per cent (this gives a precise number of customers) with new customers matching your existing long-term customer profile (which you have researched).
- To raise the company brand values.

Clearly FM could play a part in all the marketing objectives. Not all marketing objectives are best met by FM solutions. There may be problems with the product's price, distribution or physical characteristics. FM will not solve that – unless of course you wish to demonstrate the value, as a high-price product, by experiential events.

FM focuses the attention on a particular product, at a particular time, at the POS when customer behaviour with regard to awareness and experience of the brand can be influenced. FM can be planned for implementation at specific times either in support of an existing brand or brand launch or routinely repeated over a period of time.

Every FM activity must start by being related to one or more marketing objectives that will be achieved by their implementation. A clearly defined marketing objective is the justification for spending time and money on any marketing activity. Time spent in thinking through the objectives, and relating them to your overall marketing strategy, is never wasted.

Once the marketing objectives have been determined, how are they to be achieved? These objectives are achieved through use on their own or in combinations of the marketing tools available to you in what is known as the 'promotional mix'.

The promotional mix

How does FM fit with the rest of the communications mix? The promotional mix is generally divided into four different parts (see Figure 2.2).

From Tool 4 and Tool 6 (in the diagram) the available promotional activities are:

- Advertising: paid-for space and time in broadcast, print media or the new media (websites, interactive TV, SMS) and other paid-for communications. Do not forget outdoor advertising, which includes ambient and transport media in addition to posters (and balloons).
- Publicity/PR: information and opinion about your products or services carried by third parties.

- Direct marketing: both non-face-to-face and face-to-face: personal presentation to customers or prospects to which they can respond directly through filling in coupons, posting tip-ons, contacting call centres, e-mails, etc. The new media – interactive TV, text messaging and e-mails – are also a part of non-face-to-face direct marketing.

- FM and in-house selling activities: a face-to-face personal presentation of your products or services is made to customers, prospects or intermediaries carried out through retail outlets (shops), sampling, demonstrations, experiential marketing, roadshows, events, personal selling at customer premises and through merchandising and exhibitions. (Note that FM used to be considered separately from direct marketing but is now a part of it.)

- Sales promotions: incentives and offers that encourage people to behave in a particular way at a particular time and place, usually delivered by one of the other three tools.

This division of 'communications tools' within the promotional mix helps in a number of ways. It gives a rough and ready definition of what each marketing tool is able to contribute to the mix, and helps companies to decide which will be most useful in achieving particular marketing objectives. For example, an industrial company is likely to put most emphasis on direct marketing. A company requiring short-term sales may put a priority on FM to foster brand awareness and brand experience. A company with a new product (the iPhone for example) may go for publicity as its best bet . It also helps companies work out the balance between the different tools. Most of the time, there is not one tool alone that will do the job, and a balance is needed between all four. This is why it is called integrated marketing.

It is also worth keeping an eye on trends in advertising. An article in *Marketing Week* (Parker, 2006) forecasts that in 2007 internet advertising will overtake newspaper advertising (5 per cent of the £43 billion spent on marketing in the UK). It forecasts that treating the web as an add-on will be the downfall of many companies in the future. The website is a serious point of contact. Magazines have to meet ad-receptivity criteria; that is, ask: is it at the right time and place for the specialist consumer? Over 500 magazines closed and over 500 opened in 2006. With a spend on magazines of £2.1 billion and an advertising spend of £827 million magazine advertising is not dead yet, but until there is a better measurement of magazine success (rather than twice-yearly ABC figures) they will not find it easy to persuade businesses to advertise readily. *Marketing Week* forecasts it is unlikely there will be much increase in magazine advertising.

The logic of a balanced way of thinking about promotion becomes clear when you look at how promotional offers are communicated. They invariably use one or more of the other communications tools. It is rare to see a piece of direct mail without an incentive for an early reply. It is rare for companies not to try to achieve media coverage, that is publicity, of their promotions. It is increasingly common for promotions to be featured in advertising. Hybrid communications – combining sales promotions with advertising, direct mail, publicity and FM (personal selling) – are not the exception, they are becoming the rule.

For completeness, the selection of the appropriate parts of the promotional mix has a further dimension: the selection of the appropriate communication channels found from customer research. For example, advertising may be selected from the promotional mix and the press selected over TV, with newspapers preferred rather than magazines and the broadsheets selected over the 'red-tops', with the *Guardian* and *The Independent* finally chosen. These two papers would then be entered into the channel plan.

This way of thinking about the promotional mix does reflect the way FM should be used. At last it does justice to the role FM plays in building brand awareness and brand experience, enhancing customer relationships and putting across all the six Cs. At last marketing books are paying attention to FM and one day it will equal the interest and understanding of the people who have been doing the job for real for years.

The process of planning

Marketing objectives, strategies and tactics definitions

Business success is always an interplay between short term and long term, tactical and strategic. Companies succeed by thinking about tomorrow, but they fail if, in so doing, they forget about today; and the reverse is also true. The best strategy is always adaptive. The objective gives the intent: to do something. The strategy is the how and the tactic is the detail describing each activity required to achieve the strategy.

As ever there is a confusion of jargon and in FM the longer-term FM projects are sometimes called strategies (they are that sometimes), with short ones being called tactics. In this book, to differentiate them from marketing strategies and tactics, the FM long-term projects or campaigns are called ongoing, with others described as short term or a mix. A campaign is a combination of projects to achieve an objective.

In marketing:

- Marketing objectives relate to purpose, typically starting with 'to', then a verb.
- Marketing strategies relate to the method, the how, typically with 'by', then a verb.
- Marketing tactics are the detail at the activity level.

For example with a sales target set as a marketing objective, the strategy adopted may be 'by using' one or more FM disciplines. A contingent FM discipline may be employed on occasion as a tactical short-term activity, such as an FM sales team put in to support a particular outlet for a product relaunch.

The thinking behind the planning process

You should consider five points for each element of the marketing plan:

1. Understand the strategic framework in terms of competitive advantage and positioning that should underpin every FM, as any other marketing activity.
2. Establish guidelines for each product or service, determining the style of FM that will be appropriate to it. This is the same for all marketing activities.
3. Ensure that FM is handled or overseen by a sufficiently senior executive so that activities are conceived, integrated and implemented professionally.
4. Insist that FM is researched and evaluated through marketing accountability measurement in a way that enables you to assess performance, and compare it to other types of marketing expenditure.
5. Plan and budget for your use of FM over the year ahead so that the activities become integral to your marketing effort and alongside other marketing activities.

Most of this book details how to run FM activities discipline by discipline. These are the building blocks for FM planning.

The marketing plan – the outcome of the planning process

The promotional mix you select is your marketing plan. You get there by going through a business process of preparing business objectives first. Once objectives are clear then you can draw out marketing objectives and look at all the options in the promotional mix (a very large list) before picking those that you believe suit you and will achieve your objectives. The picking process (selection of the communication tools alongside communication channel planning) is helped by using a customer perspective (both existing customers and prospects) at all times and thinking throughout of the marketing mix, the six Cs, your customers' buying process and their influencers, and your brand.

Overcome the easy-life tendency

The process of drawing up a marketing plan is a useful discipline. A Willott Kingston Smith (WKS) survey found marketers relied too much on agencies to decide for them which promotional tools and channels to use. The consequence is that the promotional mix and the channels selected change little year on year. If an advertising agency is the sole supplier, beware: a number of agencies are traditionalists who have always made their money from press, poster and TV advertising. Their creative people do not have publicity, sales promotions, direct marketing (including FM) or even websites 'on their radar' and unless you insist on all parts of the promotional mix being considered, you may not really get a broad view. The WKS survey found that most agencies only pay lip service to communication channel planning. The way to overcome this is to insist on it or change to a newer agency that does.

The WKS survey also found a media buyer view that most marketers are incapable of any accountability. Do not be one of them. It is essential to measure the success of achievement of the final list you select for your plan. Allocate responsibility for each activity and objective. With the person responsible for each marketing activity, define success, then set a key performance indicator (KPI) for their marketing activity. Record the KPI and then measure it. The results indicate the success or failure of the marketing activities to allow you to make any necessary changes next time – and/or allow you to select new marketing personnel. (This is covered in detail in Mullin, 2001, *Value for Money Marketing*, Kogan Page.)

Planning is essential to achieve focus and control cost. It is a human weakness to write plans then leave them in some filing cabinet. A very short document or table is all that is required and if it is on display it will trigger the conscience. It is all too easy to forget what you originally set out to do. A plan allows you to allocate priorities in case a round of cost-cutting means a number of activities fall by the way. It will also provide a record of what you cut and how that affected the outcome when the day of reckoning comes. Equally, if the plan succeeds and the KPI is achieved you can praise and celebrate. You also have real, quantified experience for next time.

Case studies

There are not many case studies around showing integrated marketing at work and the part FM plays within it. An example of integrated marketing for Superdrug is given in the Preface. The case study below involves integration of sales promotion, POS design and production, POS distribution, retail liaison, TV, radio and FM implementation and more.

Case study: Large internet service provider (ISP) POS collation and despatch by a national handling house

Background

For each activity conducted on behalf of a large ISP, POS material including CDs, FSDUs, CTUs and leaflets are sent to FM staff for merchandising in store. All collation and despatch tasks are handled by a national handling house.

Execution

A matrix of staff with quantities for each POS item is produced by the FDS account team and sent to the handling house for collating. All POS items are sent direct to the handling house from the manufacturers to arrive two weeks prior to the activity start date. POS items are then packed according to the matrix and collected by the couriers within five days of the POS being received, usually a Friday. Delivery of POS is then made between Tuesday and Friday the following week, with the day being agreed between the courier and the consignee.

On average there are 100 different consignments made up of over 7,000 individual items. The deliveries are palletized and decanted at the point of delivery by the couriers.

Results

Delivery success is in excess of 95 per cent for each phase of the activity with any outstanding deliveries resolved within 24 hours. By despatching POS on pallets instead of in individual parcels, there are significant cost savings made with the addition of ensuring that no parcels get lost in transit.

CDs = counter displays; FSDUs = free-standing display units; CTUs = counter top units

Summary

FM is the culmination of a process. The process starts with the vision of the owners of a business or the leaders of an organization.

Typically for any year that vision is converted into SMART business objectives, of which some affect marketing directly and some affect marketing indirectly; there are a few that have little effect.

SMART marketing objectives can be derived from the business objectives. After considering the alternative marketing activities, some bundled as campaigns, choose a promotional mix to achieve the marketing objectives all set down in a marketing plan. Each marketing activity has a determinant of success set, with a KPI chosen to measure that success and achievement.

Within some of the marketing campaigns are FM activities. For each, an objective is set from which an FM brief is prepared. The brief needs to relate closely to the strategy of the company, and the response to the brief should show an understanding of how to deliver the strategy and the ability to deliver the campaign. There should also be an understanding of the measurement of the campaign, and how ROI will be judged. Planning the inclusion of FM in the marketing plan, and ensuring the quality and development of the work, will greatly aid the effectiveness of the campaigns. The subsequent added value to the brands will be marked, and could well establish a lead over the competitors.

Self-study questions

2.1. Draw from memory a diagram of how marketing fits into a business, then compare it with the first diagram in this chapter. Ensure that you have covered all the interfaces with the customer. Just how well does your business interface with the customer?

2.2. What seven 'marketing tools' does a marketer have to consider and use? Consider each of the tools and the suitability of each for the customers of your business. Remember: always start with the customer, not the business – for example, you may prefer to advertise in print as it relatively easy to arrange and visually pleases your

CEO but it is useless if your customers only use mobiles and the internet.

2.3. What is the difference between a marketing objective and a marketing strategy?

(Answers can be found in the text.)

3 What FM is and what it can do

The overriding FM benefits

This chapter looks at the kinds of marketing situations that FM best resolves from three typical perspectives – those who have prepared marketing objectives; B2B, B2C and B2P situations; and the view of the end user. Each situation is enlarged to its component parts and the appropriate FM disciplines matched to them. For example, a product launch has to cover training of in-house staff, the product should be appropriately displayed, sufficient stock must be in place, all in addition to face-to-face selling by highly trained staff at the point of launch.

The chapter deliberately sets out points in lists so it is easier to see the remedies provided by FM for the situations described.

Remember that there are five overriding benefits for all situations:

- **FM allows a client to concentrate on matters other than sales.** FM provides clients with a service that is focused on the clients' sales objectives, enabling them to spend time on their own core objectives. The service may be permanent or it may be a series of short campaigns or just a one-off. The service provides a greater control of cost. Typically it costs less than the full cost of an in-house equivalent.
- **FM can be applied wherever marketing exists.** FM operates in any environment in which marketing operates: retail, B2B and direct to the consumer. It can be applied locally, nationally or internationally. It can be

used to great effect in non-retail, B2P, including the professions and the public sector.

- **FM performs and is wholly measurable.** FM provides measurable results and in real time if required. FM is a performance-driven industry.
- **FM can provide an instant fix.** FM offers powerful, managed, flexible, short-term solutions to sales and marketing problems, for example product launches, managing pricing changes and when a pool of trained, motivated sales staff is needed for a quick fix or a crisis.
- **FM uses people.** FM is the only direct marketing discipline where the messages are delivered face to face, which means that in one meeting the FM brand ambassador can educate, influence, change opinion, correct misconceptions about the offer or the brand and persuade an end user to make a favourable purchase decision if appropriate. Using people also gives informed feedback from the end users, which often has significant value.

The FM toolbox

FM offers a dynamic and versatile service and is able to deliver successful and measured results over wide and influential sectors. It is, therefore, very disappointing that so few marketers even know about the full range of services, and often seem fixated that FM is about just sampling. It is not!

FDS – an FM agency, for example, has only around 20 per cent of its turnover for sampling each year. The other 80 per cent of the work is largely strategic, and many FDS clients will not allow FDS to showcase these strategic campaigns as they might reveal a competitive edge to their brand competitors. So, as sampling is the main discipline that tends to be in the public domain, that is what is made public and that is why people think FM is all about sampling. Please be a real, informed marketer and read on.

Brand building, brand development and CRM are achieved through the use of six main disciplines in FM, and then each discipline is subdivided; FM is far-reaching and very adaptable.

FM projects' or campaigns' duration

Just as in the rest of marketing, delivery of FM is often by projects or campaigns, and there are different types of projects or campaigns (a campaign in FM jargon is one or more projects). Note that marketing itself uses strategic and tactical objectives (see Chapter 2) which should not be confused with the FM jargon described here:

- A short-term (called in FM jargon 'tactical') campaign. A short-term FM project or campaign is one that operates within a finite time span, for example, a two-week audit, a three-month roadshow. This will meet a short-term need without disrupting a company, in a comparatively condensed time frame. The focus is on message delivery to the consumers by involving, exciting and educating them. Some short-term campaigns are one-off, others are repeated in different areas or at different times.
- An ongoing (called in FM jargon 'strategic') campaign. An ongoing FM project or campaign is on a full-time basis, and is designed to reach a large marketing target. These projects or campaigns focus on the delivery of brand strategy, and the usual length of contract is 2–3 years.
- A short-term ongoing FM project or campaign is a mix of the other two, one that runs all year, but is not full-time, such as one occupying one week a month for the whole year. Again, there is a focus on delivering strategy.

The FM toolbox of six disciplines

A reminder of the toolbox follows. Remember that a chapter is devoted to each discipline in the toolbox after this chapter. The numbers beside each discipline below indicate the chapter number for that discipline.

Chapter number and FM discipline

4. Highly targeted sales

- direct sales, short term and ongoing (known as 'tactical' and 'strategic' in FM jargon);
- door-to-door sales;
- van or car sales (sales made from a car or van);
- transfer order sales (usually for items too large or too heavy to transport in a car or van, or where there is a delivery service in place).

5. Merchandising

- POS or POP placement (not only placing the POS but also checking the correct amount of stock, replenishment, re-ordering and having correct facings in the correct place);
- building of displays (both POS and product displays);

- category management;
- crisis management.

6. Auditing

- collecting data to check in-store compliance (agreed placement, facings, POS display);
- collecting competitor activities data and subsequent analysis.

7. Sampling and demonstrating

- in-store;
- outdoor.

8. Experiential marketing, roadshows and events

- in-store;
- concourse (railway, shopping centre);
- exhibition;
- outside.

9. Mystery calling and shopping

- covert;
- overt.

Typical applications of the toolbox

Application of the FM toolbox is typically approached from any one of three directions:

- The first is planning how to achieve marketing objectives, where typical marketing objectives are examined, derived from, say, a business process such as outlined in Chapter 2, to see what might usefully be tackled by FM and which FM disciplines might be applied.
- The second direction is from that of either a B2B, B2C or B2P viewpoint, wondering what FM solutions might be available to solve what problems.
- In the third approach various users' perspectives are highlighted, considering users faced with practical tasks, asking what FM has to offer. For example, for a brand manager, at the coalface of marketing, considering what FM can do to help introduce a brand.

It should be noted that it is rare for a discipline to be used alone, usually there is an amalgamation of some of the disciplines to meet a client's specific requirements. For clarity the principles of each FM discipline are considered in detail individually in Chapters 4 to 9.

Tackling typical FM objectives

'Field marketing is the most persuasive/effective way to inform/educate customers of the features and benefits of anything that is being marketed' (Williams, 2007).

Assume that a business has gone through the process explained in Chapter 2 of establishing business objectives from which marketing objectives arise. The marketer then considers how best to achieve the objectives through marketing strategies and tactics, each consisting of one or more marketing activities. Below are some FM objectives derived from marketing objectives that FM typically addresses.

To implement a new product or service launch or a relaunch

The marketing objective may simply state that 'X (a new product) is to be launched'. You can achieve this from the toolbox as follows:

- With a new product or service you would use:
  - highly targeted sales, probably an ongoing project;
  - sampling and demonstrating;
  - experiential marketing, roadshows and events.
- At the same time, to ensure that the product is in front of the prospective purchaser, correctly placed, in prime position, with sufficient facings, correct price, correct POS accompaniment and in the proper section of the store or office, you would use:
  - merchandising.
- To see what the distribution is across the entire marketplace, multiples, independents and specialists, and to see how it compares with competitor products, you would use:
  - auditing.
- To ensure that the new product is understood by the retailers so that they can effectively communicate the brand's features, benefits and values and improve sales, you would use:
  - mystery calling and shopping (with remedial training where necessary).

- To guarantee the new product is part of a regular ordering and stocking procedure, so the brand is never out of stock, you would use:
  - merchandising;
  - auditing.
- To find out just how well the new product is selling and to monitor it on a daily, weekly or monthly basis in the field, using real time reporting, so that irregularities are spotted and sales opportunities maximized, you would use:
  - auditing.

If the client was to outsource the sales function, the FM agency would take on all these tasks.

Improving sales of an existing product or service

The marketing objective might be 'to maintain the sales to the level of the previous year'. The following FM disciplines might be applied:

- To revive and generate a deeper understanding of brand values, maintaining brand awareness with the consumer or end user, and to extend the customer base allowing the product to be sampled or trialled so as to involve and educate the end user, you would use:
  - highly targeted sales, a short-term operation or a series of short-term activities over a period of time;
  - sampling and demonstrating;
  - experiential marketing, roadshows and events.
- To support the outlets selling the brand to sell it well, with training and incentives to improve sales further, you would use:
  - merchandising (and remedial training).
- To obtain feedback to see if it is responding to market changes by 'tweaking' the activities to meet the changes, (even as the activity is running), working from the analysis of real time figures, you would use:
  - auditing.

FM for B2B, B2C and non-retail

(Note that the non-retail sector is called B2P here.)

Companies wanting professional customer relationships and engaging consumer relationships, that will push and drive their brands towards success and profits, must look to FM as a part of their strategy to achieve these goals.

What can the FM disciplines toolbox do from a business perspective? FM designs and implements face-to-face brand communications to both the B2B and the B2C sectors.

B2B

The fundamentals of brand development for B2B include:

- brand presence so that the business is aware of the benefits of the offer (product or service) so that they use or purchase it through direct sales using:
  - highly targeted sales;
  - auditing (confirming distribution);
- the visibility of the brand so that the business is aware of it for future use or purchase through:
  - experiential marketing, roadshows and events (trade shows or at warehouses or in-house events);
  - merchandising (in appropriate outlets and where warehouse outlets are used);
- a positive promotional message to encourage the business to use or buy in to the offer (the product or service) through:
  - sampling and demonstrating (at venues attended by buyers such as conferences, seminars, exhibitions).

This is supplemented, implemented and maintained by using face-to-face, well-informed CRM.

B2C

For the B2C sector, FM provides a solution for:

- brand awareness and alliance (loyalty) generation so the consumer learns about the brand and the offer – to involve, engage and educate the consumers face-to-face and to stimulate use and sales of the brand through:

- trial using sampling and demonstrating, and experiential marketing, roadshows and events;
- awareness from highly targeted sales;
- constant reminders at the POP that will ensure that sufficient quantities of the product are available for purchase and the POS display, through:
  - merchandising;
  - auditing;
- checking that in-house staff are up to speed and trained on the offer and brand through:
  - mystery shopping.

B2P

In the non-retail sector, ie business to professional bodies or persons trading, personal companies, personal agents for overseas suppliers selling into the UK, FM offers solutions. FM applied to put across the fundamentals of B2P would include:

- training of in-house staff (at all locations) in marketing (the brand, the offer – the six Cs, the sales process, the customer), CRM through:
  - highly targeted sales with training;
- confirming in-house staff training in customer focus aspects of marketing reacting appropriately to meet customer needs through:
  - mystery calling, (acting as 'members' in the case of the professions);
  - the visibility of the brand;
  - experiential marketing, roadshows and events (trade shows);
  - merchandising (all locations);
- direct sales of courses, publications or services (at events, conferences, meetings) through:
  - highly targeted sales;
  - merchandising;
- the quality of delivery of members' courses through:
  - mystery shopping;
  - auditing.

This is supplemented, implemented and maintained by using face-to-face, well-informed CRM.

For B2B, B2C and B2P

All FM projects and campaigns are conducted with the full support of experienced and structured in-house management teams, (with full business processes, supported by a cutting edge technology) that give efficient and prompt solutions and also real-time reporting.

FM – the user perspective

Who might be users of FM?

Anyone who believes marketing is about the bottom line **before** it is about interior design.

The perspective here is that of the user and three probable users with a particular problem are described by way of illustration:

- a brand manager focusing on POP and sales fundamentals;
- a sales director for a brand that needs presence, awareness and sales in the B2B market;
- a marketing manager for a brand that needs introduction to the consumers.

A brand manager focusing on POP and sales fundamentals

If a manager wants to see his or her product or service developed as a brand, more specifically by being:

- in front of the prospective purchaser, correctly placed, in prime position, with sufficient facing, displayed in the proper manner, at the correct price, with correct POS accompaniment, in the proper section of the store or office all the time, the manager would use:
  - merchandising, following a compliance agreement;
- distributed across the entire marketplace, multiples, independents, specialists, the manager would use:
  - auditing;
  - merchandising;
  - highly targeted sales;
- understood by the retailers so that they can effectively communicate the brand's features, benefits and values and improve sales, the manager would use:
  - sales training and merchandising;
  - mystery shopping;
- part of a regular ordering and stocking procedure so the brand is never out of stock, the manager would use:
  - merchandising;
- monitored on a daily, weekly or monthly basis in the field using real-time reporting, so that irregularities are spotted and sales opportunities maximized, the manager would use:
  - ongoing (strategic) merchandising and sales.

Having achieved the above, the brand manager would then want to improve sales further by:

- developing brand awareness with the consumer or end user through:
  - sampling and demonstrating;
  - experiential marketing, roadshows and events;
- generating an understanding of brand values through:
  - experiential marketing, roadshows and events;
  - merchandising;
- allowing the product to be sampled or offered for trial so as to involve and educate the end user through:
  - sampling and demonstrating;
  - experiential marketing, roadshows and events;
- selling in the product or service to end users using direct sales through:
  - highly targeted sales;
- supporting the outlets selling the brand to sell it well, with training and incentives to improve sales further through:
  - merchandising and sales;
- responding to market changes by 'tweaking' the activities to meet the changes, even as the activity is running through:
  - analysis of the results and implementation of a method for achieving better results as appropriate.

A sales director for a brand that needs presence, awareness and sales in the B2B market

A person who wants to see his or her product or service promoted, delivered or sold to the B2B market, could generate awareness by any of the following:

- direct sales B2B using:
  - highly targeted sales;
- delivering information, the product or advice using:
  - highly targeted sales;
- collecting data for permission marketing using:
  - highly targeted sales;
  - sampling and demonstrating in the B2B arena;
  - experiential marketing, roadshows and events in the B2B arena.

A marketing manager for a brand that needs introduction to the consumers

A person who wants to see his or her product or service explained, demonstrated, promoted, sold and delivered to the consumer could use the following methods:

- direct sales:
  - highly targeted sales;
- promotional activity in a public area (in store, shopping centre, motorway services or similar):
  - sampling and demonstrating;
  - experiential marketing, roadshows and events;
- sampling the product to the consumer and encouraging purchase and brand loyalty:
  - sampling and demonstrating;
  - experiential marketing, roadshows and events.

And for all three of the users above, FM can be used:

- to achieve great brand enhancing delivery:
  - with a highly trained field force;
  - with very experienced management teams;
  - by tried and tested operational systems within the FM company;
- for them to know how much the activity has delivered to the bottom line, so that effective spend can be defined as a quantifiable ROI.

But above all, one of the most important advantages of FM for all users is to be released from the day-to-day commitment of running people, training, employment, best practice, planning, and yet benefit from the advantages detailed above.

If any of the above ideas are relevant to your business and your marketing plan, then you need FM. Very few FM campaigns will use the disciplines detailed in isolation. In designing the approach for each client the disciplines are invariably integrated in order to achieve the best results and maximize the effect of the in-visit time and the face-to-face time, and thus the campaign as a whole.

However, for clarity it is easier to initially describe the disciplines separately. Now before you read Chapters 4 to 9 to obtain an in-depth understanding of each of the disciplines, there are a number of supporting disciples and ingredients, without which FM could not function.

FM staff – a key ingredient

FM staff are different form other staff. In the past the FM staff were part-time and usually women who were working to fit in with their children. This resource was very valuable, as many of these women were highly skilled professionals who were taking time out from their careers and doing FM helped them to 'keep their hand in' and earn extra money. However, despite the fact that they were very skilled for the task, the workers in FM were not always seen as having a 'proper job,' as many of the tasks required of the FM field staff were quite basic.

Over the past 15 years or so it is very different, and the calibre of FM people has changed considerably, in response to the increased client demands of the FM agencies in delivering strategy. The roles of FM staff have been up weighted, and the staff training and development greatly improved. There are more equal numbers of men and women in the industry, and many more people working on full-time strategic contracts who have top management skills. FM staff are often selected from graduates looking for their initial steps into working in sales in the field, and gaining an understanding at ground level. The training given to the people both in the offices and the field is extensive, and the standards are high. The image of the FM industry is now one of experienced people doing a skilled task.

Some points about these staff are:

- They are carefully recruited and selected.
- They are carefully administered.
- When a project is mooted the staff are selected with the clients' objectives in mind.
- They are trained and managed with bespoke management agreed for each project.

FM staff are complementary to the existing business; they are not in competition with the in-house team. After all, they both share the same objectives and desire to develop the brand successfully.

FM – the ancillaries

FM people have developed further skills from conducting the six main disciplines, which although previously and in this book are described as ancillary, in fact are now offered as supporting disciplines in their own right. These include:

- training;
- in-store staff (for more on this see Chapter 19);
- staff development;
- training of retailers on the brand;

- data management;
- technologies for data capture;
- managing data collected;
- lists;
- telephone marketing (as generally used by FM companies – not the whole discipline);
- warehousing;
- storage;
- maintaining records;
- despatch;
- fulfilment.

Details of these ancillary, supporting disciplines are given in Chapters 10 and 11.

Example of a B2B ongoing (FM strategic) contract

Provide a national team of salespeople selling utilities and telephony to businesses. Working from appointments made by telephone for them, the sales personnel visit businesses and sell the products to them, offering the businesses significant savings on what they are currently spending.

This is an ongoing exercise with a contract for two years signed with the client.

Example of a new B2C magazine product launch for consumers

The consumers were approached by 'brand ambassadors' and invited onto a stand where they received a shoulder massage or a foot massage from trained masseuses. Once they were more relaxed and had a pleasurable experience, they were offered a sample of a new women's magazine. Receiving the magazine at a time when they felt good, helped the women to associate with the magazine, which they took away with them to read and show their friends. Shops in the vicinity were well stocked with the new magazine, and sales were recorded and reported to be very good indeed.

The project repeated the event six times in six different shopping centres. This is a short-term (FM tactical) piece of work where the brand experience was positive and the brand was sampled.

Example B2P exercise for a professional body

The professional body was taking a stand at an exhibition where the numbers of people within the target market for membership were prolific. A team of three people worked on the stand, and in the exhibition generally, approaching people, asking them if they were members. They then explained the benefits of joining and aimed to sign up new members as part of a membership campaign. Names and addresses were collected to provide permission data for future contact.

With so many attendees in the right target market and in the frame of mind to consider a work related body that could offer them relevant benefits, the results of this one-off (FM-tactical) exercise were high.

Summary

From the perspectives of a user, after consideration of business circumstances and development of marketing objectives it is possible to decide which combinations of the six FM disciplines are most suited to solve marketing problems. A number of ancillary disciplines exist in support. As a generality, FM can be applied wherever face-to-face marketing situations arise.

Self-study questions

3.1. What are the overriding benefits or FM?
3.2. Which FM disciplines would you consider for a new biscuit product launch into 10,000 outlets?
3.3. Why are FM staff different?

(Answers can be found in the text.)

4 The FM sales discipline

Outsourcing to highly trained sales staff

The FM sales discipline – direct selling

Face-to-face selling is as direct as you can get. There are, however, quite different operational levels in that face-to-face encounter. The difference arises from the quality of training that any sales staff receive and of course their innate abilities that allow them to accept and put into practice that training. At a basic level there is a sales assistant only trained and capable of processing a purchase once a buyer has decided to buy, merely taking the item, placing it in a bag and accepting the means of payment. There may be perhaps an exchange of pleasantries ('Hello, can I help you?', 'Is that want you want to buy?', etc) but there is no real sales dialogue; merely a sales contact probably better described as order taking than a sale. At the other extreme is the highly trained salesperson who understands the need for sales dialogue and is motivated to obtain sales responsibly and ethically. These sales staff engage and develop a relationship with the customer taking them through the offer and the brand experience, explaining the brand values and persuading them to consider the purchase decision.

So how can mere contact or order taking be improved to become a real sales encounter? The more that the person selling knows about the buyer – the person's needs, environment, background – the more they can tailor the offer they are selling to match the needs of the buyer. The same applies to the communication used; that is, the more the seller matches the language, format, culture and social background preferences of the buyer, the more likely the messages are to be understood and acted upon by the buyer. Both the offer and communication are enhanced by the buyer's perception of the brand. If it is a strong perception then the sellers' task will be easier as the brand will encompass the offer as a series of values which have been preferentially matched and communicated to the buyer.

There is a further dimension; a seller needs to understand when the potential buyer is purchasing on behalf of someone else and why that is different. This particularly applies in B2B situations. Here the potential buyer has to be able to justify the purchase to others – the management layers above them, the owners, who may be shareholders and to their peers and subordinates. Let's call these others 'influencers'. In consequence these influencers have to be understood too. The job of the seller then is to establish where the buyer is in the firm and appreciate their capacity to respond. An owner in business can make a decision to buy on the spot. A buyer 'in the food chain' needs help – effectively acting on your behalf – to enable them to justify a purchase. A 'runner' who is sent to suss you out as a seller (for example at a trade event) needs a mass of persuasive literature to persuade the buyer to bother to see you.

Where a potential buyer is selling on to customers, knowledge of those customers has to be acquired too. For example, a client of one of the authors, supplying some 400 retail gift outlets and department stores, recently decided to sell personally at weekends directly to the public as well. The client has been amazed to discover that the truths about selling to the consumer are real, despite for many years being told that was the case. The result is now that the client is 'tuned in' to the consumer and is able to offer real support and assistance to the supplier in dealing with their own customers.

In times past sales staff were told to fact find and qualify the potential buyer. Fact finding included establishing the potential buyer's needs, background and environment and their understanding (both in terms of education and awareness) of the product or service being sold. The qualification staff needed to establish whether the buyer had the means and the sufficiency to buy; that is if they were creditworthy and authorized to purchase. This is still just as much needed today, but many seem no longer to be trained to do this, nor do they have the intention of staying with an organization or business, which means that the latter believe that it is not worth training staff as fully as they might. It is for this reason that FM is really valuable.

The FM sales discipline is concerned with highly targeted sales where the sales staff are trained to find out, understand and hold a dialogue with particular target markets. Another dimension is honesty. FM staff are ethically and socially responsible, as is described in this chapter. Such fully trained sales staff, these days, are likely only to be found in long-serving staff, who were properly trained, or those now in FM agencies.

Outsourcing

The concept of outsourcing your sales force

If you are not training your staff to really high standards, for what are now quite understandable and acceptable commercial reasons, then it is better to outsource the sales task strategically for all sales or, when it really matters, tactically, if some in-house staff are retained. Tactically FM provides the dedicated, highly trained sales force who, for example, can make a product launch take off; when you are able to target them to a particular audience.

The argument raised in the preface in this book is that, although technically face-to-face in-house sales is outside the FM disciplines, not many may know of this exclusion, and especially as FM is perceived as consisting of face-to-face disciplines, they assume it is included. Because there are face-to-face sales encounters that occur, other than with FM staff, guidance on how to improve in-house face-to-face is included in Chapter 19, which considers what might be the way to tackle raising the level of your in-house face-to-face contact with the customer. In-house staff training by the FM ancillary discipline is included in Chapter 10.

Selling for B2B and B2C clients

B2C, B2B and B2P direct sales

The sales, whether tactical or strategic can be conducted to consumers (B2C), to the business world (B2B) or to the professional (B2P), and can be executed in a wide range of venues:

- B2C sales can be made in-store, in shopping centres, in the customer's home, at shows and events, exhibitions and even in the street.
- B2B sales are more usually conducted in the customer's offices, at a trade show or an exhibition.
- B2P sales are conducted at all personal or member interfaces, at exhibitions, conferences, seminars and over the telephone.

In fact sales can usually be conducted anywhere where there is a high level of footfall of the target market for the brand. However, one thing is clear, and that is that there are likely to be rules and regulations for conducting the activity, especially if it is outside the regular, expected environments. An FM agency will advise on these regulations, and will know how to conduct the work correctly. This is important, as significant brand damage could be the result of poor planning and ignorance of the correct procedures.

There are times when events are conducted that encourage the potential customers to travel to meet the brand. For example, setting up a driving challenge at a country house to give test drives, and encourage awareness of a particular vehicle, and inviting a group of fleet managers (B2B) or targeted consumers (B2C) to visit and participate. The aim is that the visitors learn about the vehicles in a pleasant environment, which should encourage them to purchase. These events take considerable preparation (see Chapter 8 which includes event marketing). In a similar way members of professional bodies or persons in a business capacity such as self-employed (B2P) can be invited to a seminar at a place of historic or national interest which uses the occasion to inform, educate and provide brand awareness, at the same time covering a matter of interest to the audience. For example HM Revenue & Customs offer VAT seminars. Courses run at professional institution headquarters allow brand experience, brand awareness and selling opportunities.

Direct sales: strategic and tactical outsourcing

Definitions

Strategic outsourcing of sales

The strategic work is the supply of a sales force that works full time for a prolonged period (usually a minimum of two years) to achieve a client's strategic aims for his business. The FM company will supply all the staff, the complete infrastructure and all processes to conduct the entire exercise.

Tactical outsourcing of sales

The tactical work is conducted in the short term to achieve short-term objectives. The work will meet a short-term need in a comparatively condensed time frame.

Note: the third type (on-going part-time sales) rarely happens in the pure sales discipline but may in the other FM disciplines. For example, three days selling a month for one product is not always viable – a salesperson does not have enough work at this rate nor do skills develop with the product. This does happen, however, when other disciplines are mixed with the sales (e.g. merchandising and auditing) when there is more required for the task than just sales.

Strategic sales

It is becoming much more common in the UK as well as globally that many very large public corporations outsource all or part of their sales force. This means that the FM company recruits, trains and manages the entire sales force, as well as dealing with job descriptions, training, setting KPIs, personal development, pay, expenses, holidays, cars, laptops, targets, disciplinary and grievance procedures, sickness, maternity leave and more. The FM company reports into the client at a senior level, and is usually included in the strategic sales discussions on the client board (the reason for this being that the more they understand what has to be achieved, the more chance they have of delivering what the client wants).

For example, a national sales director in a major company will devote three days a month with his FM agency partner, discussing past results and future planning for the sales force, and then spend the rest of the month doing his own job, while all the time-consuming issues of running a sales force are handled by the FM company. Additionally, he will not have the fixed costs on his budgets, such as the sales team and their support costs (payroll, HR, fleet management etc) and office space, light and heat.

This also means that the FM company is handling and developing the relationship between the client and the end user of the product, often a retailer or a consumer on the brand's behalf. With a background of dealing with different products in a variety of environments, this sits well with FM.

It should be made clear that the salespeople always introduce themselves as being from the client brand, and they do not mention the FM company that actually employs them. They are, and are seen to be brand ambassadors.

Case study: strategic sales

Objective

To target specified independent off licences bi-monthly, selling in key brands such as Stella Artois and Tennents.

Dedicated sales teams were required to deliver the three critical objectives – distribution, visibility and quality (DVQ) on the biggest alcohol brands in the UK.

Process

A contract team of 18 executives, three area managers and one national field manager address the key areas of DVQ, marking a long-term commitment to the independent retail sector and maximizing sales through consistent availability of stock. For immediate implementation they carried stock of a prioritized range of products.

The flexible strategy allowed for seasonal bursts of activity, resulting in high volume throughput, supported by significant off-shelf product displays.

Innovative web-based and hand-held technology, along with unique software, enabled daily reporting, which could be readily interrogated and analysed by both partners.

Results

To date over 3,200 new distribution points have been achieved, with 26,542 POS items being placed in-store. 13,951 cases were sold and 15,019 cases placed on display between May and December and 8,983 additional chiller facings have also been gained.

Web-based reporting and analysis provides management control and immediate reporting. In addition, a coherent contact strategy has been developed.

The case study above shows the volumes that can be achieved and behind this there will also be mechanisms that will show ROI, the levels of profit, improved capabilities and other measurable benefits. Clearly these measures are confidential to the client who has been generous in allowing the case study to be used as an example of a strategic contract.

A number of senior organizations have adopted outsourcing to FM companies as the way forward, as it brings a flexibility that would be impossible internally, and offers greater controls on costs. If a client counts the costs of the in-house sales force and includes not only the sales team costs, but also the support that the people need, such as payroll, HR, fleet management, personnel issues (including staff development), training, etc, and the cost of heat, light, space and equipment, then an outsourced sales force will cost up to 15 per cent less than an internal one, and will provide an enhanced and robust service for this lesser cost. The FM sales forces are very focused on delivery, and with the will to deliver front of mind, the motivation and drive within these sales forces is truly remarkable, as these senior organizations recognize. This is evidenced in their continuing use of FM for many years.

There are times when the client may turn to outsourcing a sales team when there are current workers in this area of the business. These workers can be transferred to the outsourced company via the Transfer of Undertaking of Permanent Employment (TUPE). While this involves specific processes including consultation with the employees and careful HR management, FM companies will help conduct this process.

An FM company can draw on expertise across many different accounts. This not only brings different learning experiences, but it also motivates staff to do well, as they can move on more quickly, either to another account for promotion, or even into a client 's direct employ, which has been effected successfully several times at FDS.

It is also true that an FM company will be able to create and establish a sales force more quickly than the client itself, as the management and the processes will largely be in place. For some clients this time saving has been crucial in stealing a march on their marketplace.

Supplying staff at this level is clearly ongoing, with a contract signed for usually a minimum of two years, and this would apply to door-to-door sales, which are also undertaken by FM companies.

Case study: B2B

Objectives

To increase the market penetration of Business Link services in Milton Keynes, Oxfordshire and Buckinghamshire. To raise the satisfaction level achieved from those using Business Link's services and to increase the number of small and medium-sized enterprises (SMEs) taking up and benefiting from professional business advice.

Process

FDS supply and manage a team of nine account managers on behalf of Business Link Solutions, the Business Link operator for Milton Keynes, Oxfordshire and Buckinghamshire. The account managers are responsible for supporting and encouraging growth in the local SME community. Business Link Solutions supplies approximately one third of the required leads; the FDS team generate the remainder from networking and cold calling.

Initial calls to businesses involve a 1 to 2 hour face-to-face meeting to discuss the business objectives, the management team's aspirations and their current position in four key areas; marketing and sales, finance, operations and HR. A plan of action is agreed, detailing the management's medium-term objectives and the key issues to be addressed over the coming months.

The action plan may involve advice and assistance of a third party, further training for the business staff or a reorganization of resources within the company to effectively address and resolve the issues identified.

Results

586 businesses have been 'substantially assisted' between January and March, in comparison to 101 businesses in the same period in the previous year, prior to FDS' involvement.

Over the same duration the FDS team have contacted 835 businesses on behalf of Business Link Solutions, comprising both new companies and follow-up calls to existing clients, up 196 per cent on last year.

To conclude, the first quarter saw 643 face-to-face meetings take place, an increase of 246 per cent on the same period the year before.

Door-to-door strategically outsourced sales

FM companies have made significant gains for clients in the door-to-door arena, and are able to deliver high results, but equally important is the quality of work.

In some sectors of the door-to-door arena, there has been significantly bad press, and it is indicative of the benefits of outsourcing that the very poor standards, which undoubtedly featured in the field, were not experienced within FM companies. There are two main reasons for this:

An FM company understands brand protection – after all the positive promotion of a brand is the main point of all the work they conduct, and so the FM companies will have tried-and-tested systems and processes for managing the staff and ensuring the quality of sale

FM companies work door-to-door sales on a 'cost plus' contract, which means that the salesperson is salaried and is therefore an employee. As an employee the salesperson must obey the company rules and regulations, including the standards and quality of the sales process. Salaries are low with a commission element based on good practice and sales volume to reach a good 'on target earning' (OTE). It is mostly in the commission-only areas that the reported bad practice took place, the commission-only salesperson is self-employed and is responsible only to himself or herself. He or she has no 'cushion' of the basic wage, which, although low, deters the tendency to pressure sales or mis-selling.

Of course the client might wish a commission-only arrangement as there is no risk to the client in this situation, but the commission-only system leaves the sales company and their self-employed agents with **all** the risk. FM companies have found that where the risk is shared, the results are better for all in terms of sales, results, standards and quality and ultimately, of course, the PR for the client also. This shared risk also encourages the client to deliver objectives and demonstrate commitment by completing actions in a timely and efficient manner.

Large companies need to protect their reputations in these areas and need to consider the huge risk to their results, image and brand by trying to cut corners. The situation requires careful handling which the larger FM companies are resourced and experienced to deliver.

The FMC best practice guidelines

These guidelines provide the following advice for the times when field personnel are required to visit members of the public in their homes.

Members of the FMC should ensure that they show a due sense of responsibility for these staff, and for the public. This will involve the following (although not exclusively):

- Staff should be vetted carefully to ensure that they are suitable to visit the public in their homes; references should be obtained and followed through very carefully.
- All staff must be supplied with a photographic identification badge with details of a telephone number and contact point to enable the householder to telephone a help desk to check the validity of the agent if they feel it is necessary.
- The company should ensure that all staff are working in a suitable area in a team, particularly in relation to women working in the evenings. It is also recommended that visits should not be carried out after 8.00 pm unless by previous arrangement.
- The company should ensure that the specific training is carried out for that project depending on the brief received from the client, ie product knowledge tests or sales training. This will include clear statements being made to verify that the customer has understood what he or she has purchased and the commitment the customer has undertaken.
- Codes of conduct should be developed in conjunction with the client as guidance for the field staff when dealing with customers, and should be understood and adhered to at all times.

Case study: B2C door-to-door sales

Objective

To conduct door-to-door sales to the consumer for gas and electricity.

Activity

Sales staff were recruited and highly trained in sales, as well as in the ethical approach with strong codes of conduct. An efficient back office monitored all the sales and registered these. The quality of sale was endorsed with checks to the consumers to ensure that they were happy with the sale. Complaints were monitored, and these were a fraction of the average national complaint ratio thanks to the stringent controls on staff, excellent training and constant monitoring. At its peak this programme employed over 350 people.

Results

In a three-year period over 750,000 sales were effected in three counties of England.

Other sales solutions

Strategic or tactical sales

A client requiring more distribution, increased sales, or a pull-through from the distributors for its products, either nationally, or in a specific region, might look at either a long-term strategic campaign or a short-term tactical sales solution to the relevant issues in the independent retail sector.

These short-term solutions often have differing names such as 'blitz activity', 'van or car sales', 'Commando sales forces' to name a few. These all offer the same service in that a short-term sales solution can be implemented. The term 'van or car sales' activity is not so well known and this is where staff sell product, usually as part of a special deal, from the back of the car or van to independent retailers to gain distribution.

Sales can also be achieved for a client through a 'transfer order' being taken by the salesperson. This order will then be sent to the distributors, for example a brewery or a delivered wholesaler, either electronically or by fax and the distributors will then fulfil the order direct to the customer as part of their regular delivery service.

For any short-term sales solution, the client should bear in mind that salespeople working for FM companies are not going to be out of work if they are good at their jobs, so some weeks are needed to plan the campaign, so that the best calibre people can be reserved for the activity. The top salespeople will not be sitting idly by waiting for the client to call! Nevertheless, FM companies keep up-to-date lists of sales personnel and ensure that they do not lose top performers by maintaining good relationships through management, training and a constant flow of work.

Sales from van or car

These are also known as ex-car or ex-van sales. When wishing to increase distribution in the retail sector a tried and tested method of achieving this is to sell the product to the retailer from the back of the van or car driven by the salesperson. The salesperson will talk to the business manager or owner and sell the features and benefits of the product he or she is carrying, sell the product and then merchandise it on the shelves before leaving.

This is an excellent way of achieving better distribution, and higher visibility for the brand, and the salesperson will need to be able to talk to the retailer in terms of margins that can be made from the product, and the benefits that stocking that product will bring to the retailer.

This type of work does carry a warning. The sales will be increased through the activity, but the independent retailers are fickle and will switch to another product should that come with a special offer. The gains do not stick for long unless there is a continuous programme of support for the retailer in place. For example, if the retailer maintains a certain level of display and product stock, then the next time a brand ambassador visits, they can be rewarded, perhaps with free stock.

Example of product erosion

The chart following shows the results from an exercise with an FMCG client where:

- An audit was conducted to get the base.
- Five visits were then made, and these show the growth as the relationship develops over the period.
- The stores were then not visited for eight weeks.

The chart demonstrates how important it is to maintain a relationship through visiting – and the impact that has when visits stop.

The advantages of ongoing 'callage' in the independent sector can be set out as follows:

Sell in → Establish relationship, sell features and benefits → Gains distribution.

Best display → Increases rate of sale → Incentive.

Category advice → Increases retailer income → Commitment from retailer.

Retailers are often offered an incentive reward to maintain the stocks and the displays. This reward should always focus on what is visible or available on entry to the store, as this ensures that customers are always ready to shop.

This type of exercise can be conducted either as a long-term strategic exercise to maintain constant advantage or executed with tactical work, which can be turned on and off.

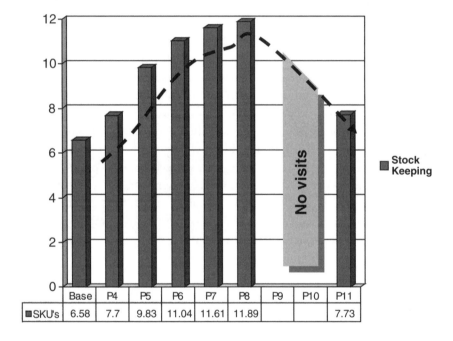

	Base	P4	P5	P6	P7	P8	P9	P10	P11
■SKU's	6.58	7.7	9.83	11.04	11.61	11.89			7.73

Results

Stock keeping units (SKUs):

Average SKUs at the start of the test   6.58

Average SKUs after five visits   11.89

Average SKUs after eight weeks of no visits   7.73 (4.16 SKUs down on average)

78% of the gains made were eroded in the eight-week period.

While the final position at the end of the eight-week period is not as far down as the start position of the initial audit, this chart shows the need to maintain a presence to maximize the significant value that the independent retailer can deliver for a brand.

Figure 4.1 Impact of visits on growth
Source: FDS

Retailer incentives for car sales

For any distribution drive there needs to be a very good offer on the products. The independent trade in particular will expect the offer, as this is the incentive for them to purchase. Regular offers include three cases for the price of two, and high discounts at 25 per cent and more are quite usual. It is, however, best to sell the product at the regular cash and carry price, and provide incentives with additional items, for example stock, as this gets the retailer used to buying and selling the product at the correct price.

Promotions are often devised specifically as an incentive to the retailer to purchase the product in good quantities or buy a range of goods, often at specific times of the year, for example beer just prior to Christmas, ice cream just prior to summer, chocolate before the return to school or prior to Easter. This will develop the retailer's loyalty with the brand, as the retailer gains sales and works towards the incentive.

Retaining the distribution and sales

If the distribution is to be retained and even improved upon, then regular visits to the same outlets will help to maintain this high level of distribution. A real relationship is developed with the retailer, and the brand becomes one of the retailer's 'must stock' lines, and thus is available for all the customers to purchase.

This ongoing relationship will also increase the sales and also the visibility, and hence the sales over long periods of time, which will not only gain awareness and acceptance with the consumers, but also deliver profits to the bottom line.

Car sales should focus on gap fill and new listings and not try to replace the route to market.

Transfer order sales

There are times when it is not possible to sell stock ex-car or ex-van due to the product, and on these occasions a transfer order may be taken. For example, a drinks product in cans or in bottles is very heavy for a car, and even a van has a limited weight allowance. Thus if such a product is to be introduced to a pub, for example, the landlord or landlady receives the visit, samples the product, checks the price and the margin he or she can make, and then places an order. This order would be written on a transfer order sheet, which is then faxed to the brewery. The brewery will then fulfil the order via its regular deliveries to the pub.

Food service

This is an area of sales where the transfer order is used all the time. Food service is the selling in of a range of products to an outlet where you can purchase food and drink and consume it on the premises.

There are four main types of food service:

- education – schools, colleges and university canteens or restaurants;
- healthcare – hospitals, nursing homes;
- business and industry (B & I) – office and factory canteens and restaurants;
- other – anywhere else that has a restaurant or cafeteria – pubs, zoos, museums, leisure centres, parks, travel terminals, etc.

Generally the work will be conducted in each area in support of a specific depot, and the transfer orders written are sent to the depot to deliver to the outlet. This has benefits for both the brand and the wholesaler or depot:

- The products being sold are listed in the outlets and gain distribution and sales.
- The depot gains more sales from their food service customer.
- The depot gains new customers as the salespeople make new contacts and sales.

This type of work requires a salesperson who can vary his or her sale according to the outlet visited, as the products presented to the outlet will vary by demographic of the outlet, for example the range of foods sold to the cafeteria for *Woman's Weekly* magazine would be different from the range sold to Ford's at Dagenham, and schools are now seeking healthier options. The client too, has to recognize these differences and allow a wide portfolio of products where possible, that can be varied according to the call.

The salesperson will visit the outlet, give samples for trial of the products he or she is promoting, seek sales of the product, sign a transfer order form with the outlet manager, and if the product is stocked in the outlet, check the stocking of the product – often to planogram and merchandise the shelves.

In this type of sales there are severe restrictions on the hours that can be worked, for example, the outlets are busy at lunchtime and cannot be visited between 11.30 am and 2.30 pm, and for many of these visits an appointment will have to be made. This means that a salesperson can achieve fewer calls in a day.

This work is also about building relationships for the brand, to increase sales by introducing new products or new product varieties, checking compliance in the areas where there is a self-service part of the cafeteria, and developing extra sales for the brands and the nominated wholesaler or depot.

This type of exercise is a strategic exercise so that gains can be made, outlets won over and the client's sales developed to a sustainable business.

The following case study features a campaign designed by the FM agency to push sales that:

- was seasonal – set up in October to meet Christmas demands;
- was achieved through ex-car sales;
- carried a retailer incentive;
- centred on merchandising displays.

Case study: Christmas Space Race

Objective

To achieve maximum visibility for Stella Artois and Tennents in Scotland and to block competitor display space during the crucial trading period to Christmas.

Process

During the period up to Christmas the DVQ team encouraged retailers throughout the UK to take part in the Christmas Space Race. Giving them the responsibility of purchasing key SKU's to create floor displays, featuring a mix of canned and bottled packs, including a minimum of five cases of six packs. Retailers were also encouraged to enhance displays with appropriate POS.

Each retailer complying with the set criteria received a free case of Stella Artois Large Can and the best display within each of the 18 territories won a stocked Husky double door chiller. Nationally the best display received a Citroen Relay van.

Results

A total of 502 outlets participated in the activity resulting in 1,798 cases being sold – the equivalent of £26,970 in sales value. Secondary displays appeared in 1,322 outlets.

Mr Faldu, the overall winner, commented that as a result of having the display in his Bolton store multi-pack sales soared from zero to an average of 20 cases per week.

Summary

Highly trained people who are selected to match the target customers, and equipped with a full knowledge of the offer and brand values, are at an advantage to make sales. This is self-evident and recognized by the businesses that outsource the sales function to FM agencies. That these salespeople should be deployed where there is a high density of prospects is important in order to recoup and exceed their cost. In direct sales where FM staff are dealing with independents the importance of seizing every opportunity to sell in and in retaining the visits can be demonstrated. Full outsourcing of the sales function allows a business to concentrate on its core business.

Self-study questions

4.1. What are the benefits to a client of outsourcing sales?
4.2. What are the key management issues for door-to-door sales?
4.3. What are the main outlets for food service?

(Answers can be found in the text.)

5 The FM merchandising discipline

If the product is not on the shelf, it cannot be bought. (Williams, 2007)

The merchandising discipline

If a brand is not on the shelf, or not visible, it cannot be bought, which makes merchandising a crucial part of proclaiming product or service presence, and in ensuring good placement, correct pricing and product availability in sufficient quantity to meet demand and drive sales.

Merchandising is also a very important part of brand awareness and the purchasing environment for the consumer – after all, 70 per cent of purchasing decisions are made in-store. It involves making sure that the brand is obvious and available – it will generate sales by:

- placing POP or POS material in an outlet to promote the product;
- stacking the shelves to the correct number of products or varieties and number of facings so that availability is obvious;
- placing self-talkers advertising the product;
- building a secondary display, for example a free-standing display in an aisle, or a display on a gondola end in-store;
- installing a special promotion and placing all the communication for the activity;

- meeting with the staff in-store and promoting the brand to them, checking their ordering procedures and ensuring that systems are in place to avoid running out of stock.

The amount by which sales will be uplifted by merchandising activity will vary according to the product, position and environment, but, as a guideline only, a secondary display in a grocery multiple can lead to a minimum of 25 per cent uplift in sales and frequently much more, depending on the product.

Merchandising can be a tactical or a strategic ongoing activity with regular POP materials replaced and updated, and this ensures that promotions and products are communicated with impact.

If you have followed the process so far, you will understand the crucial ingredients in devising a well considered merchandising campaign and its value in the sales process.

Definition

Merchandising is the placement of POS or POP materials such as posters and shelf barkers in a retail environment. However, the FM merchandising discipline has extended, becoming somewhat of a hybrid, borrowing parts of the elements from other disciplines, to include:

- visiting a retail outlet, establishing a rapport with the retailer (CRM);
- discussing the retailer's stocks of the brand, the presentation of the brand and discussing the profit the retailer can expect from the brand (sales);
- selling some of the product to the retailer, either from the merchandiser's car or by taking a transfer order (sales);
- merchandising the product on the retailer's shelves (merchandising);
- conducting an audit to highlight the status of the brand in that outlet on entry and exit defining the achievements of the call (auditing).

If merchandising calls of the hybrid type are conducted with the same retailer on an ongoing basis as part of a strategic contract, the rapport becomes stronger and more brands or product variants can be sold in to the retailer, extending the reach of the brand.

By including so many steps in the visit, the outputs from the visit are maximized, which makes the best use of the merchandiser's time and, therefore, the budget.

The merchandising task

A typical merchandising day schedule

The merchandising is conducted very differently in multiples and independent stores, so these are dealt with separately.

Independent stores

A merchandiser to the independent stores will conduct between 8 and 20 or so calls per day depending on the objectives and content of the call, the size of the stores and the distance between the stores.

The merchandiser will have a list of the stores to be visited and a journey plan to follow, so that the best routes are taken and the mileage is kept to a minimum. Generally speaking, a merchandiser would expect to act as a salesperson when they might also carry stocks and sell these in. Having explained the product to the manager and sold it to him or her, the merchandiser will then place the stock on the shelves, cleaning and tidying the shelves, and also placing the POS appropriately. A merchandiser might also negotiate a better display position or more space. Records would be kept, so that the next visit is well targeted and appropriate.

Multiple stores

Before setting out the merchandiser would acquire the store order history, display plan (planogram) and have previously cleared the visit timings. On arrival at the outlet the merchandiser reports to the manager or store security. The merchandiser then checks the display to confirm the facings are displayed according to the planogram, cleans the display and any POS material, refilling shortfalls in the display to a stocking plan from the stock held in the warehouse. The merchandiser then discusses the ordering with the category manager, checking the sales out, out of stocks and book stock errors (see 'Category management' below).

Depending on the task in hand the merchandiser would be expected to cover about 6–10 stores a day, this will also depend on the distance between stores.

For all types of store

While in the store the merchandiser might take photographs of the work done (before and after) and might also record the details required on a report, or a system that will give real-time reporting (see Chapter 11, which explains methods of data capture).

Merchandisers also report on competitors, display, facings and POS, noting their position in the store. Merchandisers from time to time meet the salespeople to discuss possibilities (where the salesperson is a different individual, mostly nowadays the merchandiser will also sell into smaller outlets), especially when new products are to be sold in.

A merchandiser should have category and product information that will give advice on the best display and range for an outlet. A good FM company will grade the outlets and score against size, sales, position, for example near a school, size of range of products, etc, and this will help the merchandiser to know what sells best in what outlets. A merchandiser is a valuable source of feedback on an outlet, dramatically enhanced by the data that the merchandiser can now technically acquire on each visit.

Category management

A category is the range of products of the same type or function that are displayed in a supermarket. For example, laundry products are all displayed in the same aisle, as are cleaning products, biscuits, etc.

In the major multiple retailers, there is a planogram for each category, the location of each brand is negotiated and this may even require some investment from the supplier. However, the placing does not just mean that the highest bidder gets the prime location. Research has shown that if the best sellers for a category are placed in the prime position, then the sales for the

Figure 5.1 Before and after

entire category can rise considerably, so getting the planogram right is important.

For example, in the 1990s, Nestle advocated best sellers in prime positions in both the multiple and the independent stores, and this resulted in the sales for the total confectionery category to increase by 21 per cent.

The prime position will vary according to the shop and the layout of that shop. Generally speaking, in a supermarket with aisles the prime location is at eye level in the busy traffic aisles.

In the independents there is no specific positioning in store, but even so the retailers are often aware of what sells best and where it should be sited, and some brands will offer incentives to the retailer if their prime placing is maintained. For example, for a display tray of confectionery products placed to the right of the till, the prime location is the bottom left-hand corner from the customers' point of view, and the closer to this point the better, the worst location being the top right-hand corner.

Compliance

Once the planogram has been agreed, it is important that the products are where they should be, and that the store display is compliant with the plan. The following is an example of free-standing display unit (FSDU) compliance in a store group. This is a real example (although extreme):

- No support – the FSDUs were delivered to the stores and the stores were to place them and merchandise them. The results when this occurs have

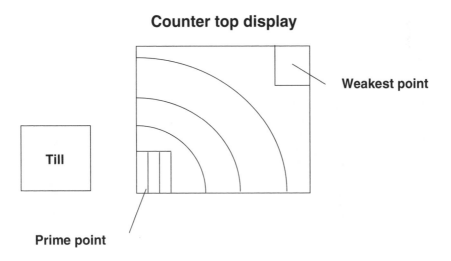

Figure 5.2 Planogram

been found to be as low as 32 per cent and at very best 65 per cent – thus 48 per cent is the average compliance for no support.

- FM support – the FSDUs were sent to the store and FM merchandisers placed them and merchandised them. This is a better situation, but there is still a gap where stores cannot find the FSDUs, they are lost, damaged or have been shredded.
- FM delivery and support – the FM merchandisers took the FSDUs to the store, placed them and merchandised them, clearly showing the improved compliance when FM control the whole process. Ideally the FM agency would wish to reach 100 per cent, but this is not always possible if the store manager will not agree, or the shop is too small to accept the FSDU for example.

In order to gain compliance a certain number of steps have to be executed. These are called the sales fundamentals in the FM industry, and are:

- Increase agreed distribution.
- Improve agreed displays.
- Gain store compliancy.
- Build store relations.
- Build agreed displays.
- Support store or regional activity.

In working for a brand in store to establish compliance there are three stages:

1. Sales fundamentals:
    - book stock errors (where the store 'book' states that the store has stock, but there is none);

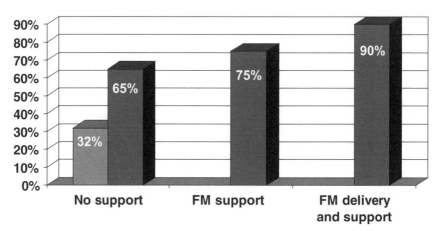

Figure 5.3 Example of FSDU compliance

- shelf edge labels (they are there and in the correct place);
- out of stocks (there is none in stock);
- position and planogram;
- management of stock (stock is out on the shelves, there is plenty in the stockroom).

2. Pre-sell activity:
    - influencing the case orders (especially where out of stocks occur);
    - agreeing display space.

3. Display:
    - implementing in store;
    - placing POS materials.

The merchandiser will work through the three stages, if the job requires it, for their brand.

Compliance is good for both the store and the supplier of the brand, and there are three main points to remember about compliance:

- There should be clear definitions between the retailers and the suppliers on compliance, so that there is clarity on what products should be in place and where.
- The FM support must be supportive of the store and its head office's agreed aims.
- All parties must use the data collected to maintain agreements, drive change and improvement.

Measuring compliance

Having negotiated a location in the multiple, then the supplier of the brand will want to be sure that the agreement the supplier has made with the head office is being implemented at store level.

A merchandiser going into a multiple will measure how well that store is doing by measuring against the agreement that the brand has with the store head office. The merchandiser can also use electronic POS data so that he or she is aware of issues prior to calling at the store. The issues include:

- sales out (sales made in-store);
- out of stocks (ie if the product was not available);
- book stock errors (where the book for the store says the brand is in stock, but the fact is that there is none in the warehouse, and it is out of stock).

If a product has been out of stock on the shelves, then the merchandiser also needs to work out why this is. There could be three main reasons:

- There is just not enough product in-store and the store has run out.
- There is not enough space allocated to the brand, and it is selling out on the shelf more quickly than the store staff are able to replenish the shelf. In this case more facings of the product would be the best answer if it is possible.
- Book stock error, as described above.

Research conducted in a grocery multiple store

Figure 5.4 gives a clear visual view of the effects of not visiting stores and giving the support to the retailer.

Broadly speaking the lines pointed out on the chart show where the sales were not made. And no lines mean that sales were made. The top part of the chart was from data collected at stores that were regularly visited. The bottom half of the chart shows the data from stores that were not visited.

Reporting on category management

It is critical that the reports on any non-compliance in major multiples is quick and accurate, as out of stock for a brand might prove a significant loss

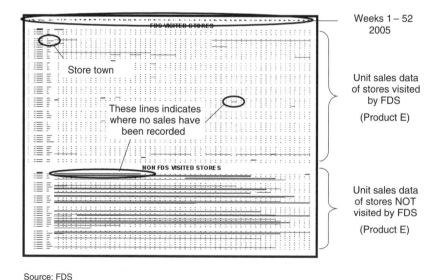

Source: FDS

Figure 5.4 Effect of field visits

of sales in a matter of hours, let alone days. The swift electronic reporting (see Chapter 11) is a real advantage here. For example, one client needed displays built in-store, which had to be executed within very tight timelines to be ready for expensive TV campaigns to support the initiative. The top 500 stores were visited on day 1 before noon, and well before noon there were stores not compliant, and the agency and the client were aware immediately. The client contacted the stores' head office and started corrective procedures there and then. Before noon of day 1 it was clear that 20 per cent of stores were non-compliant, but all issues were in hand and were being corrected.

Relationship and sales development

In an ongoing merchandising activity a large part of the success will be the development of the relationship with the retailer, so that the retailer builds an understanding of the brand and its requirements. The repeat visits will not only gain extra facings, improved stock control and better visibility for the product; they will also ensure that these remain in place, so that the sales pull-through is constant. This level of activity can pay dividends for the client. FDS have examples of merchandising activities that have returned over £4 for every £1 spent, and it is very common to achieve over £2 for every £1 invested. (See Chapter 14 on ROI.)

The merchandising activity can be flexed to meet the client peak sales periods; for example alcohol just before Christmas and ice cream in summer. The calls can be more regular in these peak times, and thus help the retailer to gain the best sales possible, which also helps the brand to maximize its sales opportunities.

When working with a merchandiser's call file of stores and visiting them, it is possible to categorize the stores into, say, the A, B and C stores. The aim throughout the period of work would be to ensure that the A stores are performing very well, and work to get B stores performing well so that they can be uplifted into the A category, and the C stores into the B category. In this way there is a constant push to move the strategy forward to achieve the best possible results in each store. Visits can be scheduled according to the sales from the stores, and one group could, for example, be visited weekly, the next group fortnightly, the third group monthly and so on, thus keeping the level of costs in line with the production and potential of each store.

By categorizing the stores, the potential for each store can be assessed (volume of sales, size of store) and each retailer can be helped to realize that potential. Then you have a win-win situation.

In assessing the potential of each store, it is important to have data that is meaningful. For example, it would be a waste of money to send out display units for all the stores, when many will not have the space to place them. The data on the stores needs to be up to date, accurate and centrally stored so that it can be investigated and manipulated as required. For example for a product that sells well to young people, stores near colleges and universities might be sought.

The data for the outlets can be captured in considerable detail using the extensive and sophisticated methods that are described in Chapter 11 on technology and data capture.

Placing POS or POP materials

Merchandisers should be trained to know where they can place the POS. Generally speaking, common sense will prevail with experienced staff. If the POS is placed where it is in the way and becomes damaged, it will be taken down by the outlet manager or owner and that defeats the object of the exercise. Often managers will know where they want the POS placed, and providing this meets the objectives of the campaign. This is a good option as the POS is unlikely to be moved. If the manager wants the POS placed in an inappropriate position, then the merchandiser must negotiate, explaining that the POS will raise the profile of the brand and drive sales. Depending on the outlets to be visited, there are not always hard and fast rules for the sites in which the POS can be placed.

Consistent shop style and image

Many groups of businesses, including franchised businesses, require that all the stores follow a very specific style and placement of their POS and special offers. Often the brand managers for these chains find that the consistency does not work well when they rely upon the store owners to implement the POS placement.

FDS worked for a large fast food restaurant chain that changed all its POS throughout each of its outlets once every month. FDS only has three days in any one month to visit all the restaurants and make them all compliant by implementing all the changes to the posters and advertising materials throughout each outlet, including the on-table offers and posters in the corridors. This is the only way that the consistency and accuracy of the POS and the 'look' of the franchises can be achieved, so that there is conformity through the chain, and all of this must be completed within the strict timescales. The activity was always timed to be in place for a TV advertising campaign set around a specific TV programme on a Thursday, so that the public would see it all in place on the Friday when they were in-store.

Dealing with merchandising crises

Crisis management

There are occasions when there is a crisis with a product, for example incorrect labelling or a health hazard with a food product. This sort of activity does not happen very often, but when it does it needs to be dealt with very quickly. The products must be removed from the shelves as quickly as is humanly possible.

In the multiple outlets this can be dealt with through head office advising all the stores to remove the product immediately, so this is relatively straightforward. However, in the independent sector it is more difficult.

If there is ongoing strategic work being conducted for the brand, then the brand stockists are known, and there is a sales or merchandising force out there ready to call on all the outlets. If there is no ongoing work, then a blanket visit has to be made to all independent retailers, and a crisis merchandising team has to be put together very quickly.

The merchandisers will visit the stores (often with a hired van) and take the offending product out of the store. They must then give the store owner or manager either cash for the product they are taking, or a voucher stating how much stock has been removed and its value, so that the store can be compensated by the brand in the next few days.

If the product problem is that the labelling is incorrect, and the application of a new label solves the problem, then the merchandisers could visit the store, relabel the product found in the store, and that is the end to the problem.

While the rest of this book asks clients to allow time for planning so that an exercise goes well, clearly there is not time to plan for the crisis once a serious situation has arisen. The job will be done, and the public will be protected as quickly as possible, but the client should not expect every aspect of the task to go smoothly, with no time to plan some aspects will not, so be prepared for some difficulties.

Tips for merchandising

Tips for building or placing POS materials

POS placement is usually an important part of a merchandising exercise, and there are several tips on this score:

- The POS should be in keeping with the average size of the store: there may simply not be sufficient room for larger pieces in some stores.
- If larger pieces of POS are being developed, they must be able to fit in a car, otherwise the distribution costs will be high.
- Banner posters hanging from the ceiling and shelf wobblers can set off the alarms in some stores; make sure there are alternative pieces of POS in case a manager points this out to the merchandiser.
- Merchandisers need a full toolkit to place POS, including adhesive, invisible string, scissors, sharp knife and even washing-up liquid, a bucket and a sponge. Depending on the POS, ladders will be required if any items are to be placed up high.
- The training needs to include health and safety, especially lifting, both for the operative and for the customers in the venue at the time of the placement.
- Training to place the posters needs to be given too. For example, there is a specific knack to gaining good placement of a sticky-backed window decal. This is best done with soapy water and a sponge, and it requires a lot of practice at the training session.
- Placing POS takes time to be done correctly and to a high standard, the number of calls a day will need to be considered carefully.
- The time of the call might be relevant too. Large banners hanging from the ceiling in a store may have to be placed after 7.00 pm when the store is closed to avoid inconveniencing the customers – and it's much more difficult now that the stores are open for longer hours.
- There will be difficulties when a large central display is built in an aisle. The area will be filled with product while the display is built, and considerable care and store rules must be followed to avoid injury or disruption to a customer.
- If the POS is large, then either vehicles must be hired to accommodate the POS or staff booked who have the larger cars – although booking staff for the size of their car might not be the correct motivation for a quality job!
- Practice in building complicated FSDUs should be conducted at the training before the work begins. Some of these can be quite difficult to understand the first time they are built as the instructions are not always clear.
- There should always be a set of POS materials at head office, and people answering questions from the field need to have practised putting the complicated pieces up too, so that they can answer questions if anyone phones in.

- Above all, the POS must be clean and tidy, placed correctly (ie straight and even and appropriately) and not adhered to the outlet walls with adhesives that will stain and are not easily removed.

Any supplier (client of an FM agency) reading this should note that on average 60 per cent of POS material sent direct to the retail venue for placement ends up lost in a corner or in the shredder. The field staff should be sent the materials and they should go into each store with them; this is the only way in which the POS will be correctly placed in every outlet (providing the store manager does not refuse its placement, which very occasionally happens).

Summary

The merchandiser is the eyes and ears of the supplier on the ground. The two-way benefit of merchandising ensures that the product is constantly available, displayed in the manner agreed with POS, with facings and shelf edge labels compliant, stock replenished and available and of merchantable quality. The merchandiser should feed back any problems encountered by managers or staff. The mantra 'if the product is not on the shelf it cannot be bought' encapsulates the role of the person who ensures that it all happens at the face-to-face point of product and customer; the merchandiser.

Self-study questions

5.1. What are the three crucial parts of merchandising that proclaim product presence?

5.2. What are the three stages of checking for compliance?

5.3. What crises can merchandising deal with?

(Answers can be found in the text.)

6 The FM auditing discipline

For anyone responsible for a brand and its development, knowing the status of your brand is an important part of planning the steps that can then lead up to improvement and increased visibility, availability and sales. An auditing campaign could, for example, track a product or a product range through 10,000 outlets and from the results a way forward would be clear that ultimately would provide the strategy that would improve the sales. Equally, auditing is an excellent way of knowing what improvements have been made, as future results can be then be measured against any earlier status. The initial status, present status and the history of any in-between status will clearly show how the product is performing.

Definition

Auditing is the recording of information on a brand to establish its position in a marketplace. For example, visiting a range of retail outlets and recording the presence of the brand means that you can establish the distribution, presence and availability of that brand. Analysis can then be conducted that will show the results, and establish a way forward to improve those results, or maintain them if they are positive.

The most common use of auditing is for:

- Compliance. Is the product where it should be on the correct shelf?
- Call grading. With graded calls the potential of an outlet is understood, and this can be developed.

- Measuring a test, for example a new display or a new planogram.
- An incentive for the retailer if the retailer's compliance is maintained over a period of time.

An excerpt from a day in the life of an auditor

I have a number of audit calls to be completed today so it's time to get into the car and program the visit address into the SAT NAV and I am on the road.

Arrive at first call and park up making sure I have my PDA (which I charged last night) and other equipment needed to complete the call.

Time to introduce myself to the owner of the store and advise him of what the purpose of my visit is today.

First on the list is to check which products are available on the shelf to purchase from my client's ranges, then I need to count the number of facings of each of our products.

I also need to count all of the competitor product facings with the specified categories (this will then allow the office team to calculate what share of space our client's brands have in each store).

Time to take the tape measure out of my bag and measure the length of each of the shelves. I am getting some funny looks from some of the customers – they look a bit confused because I have a tape measure.

All I need to do now is count the number of shelves, and thank the retailer for his time.

Outside the shop I complete the final details into the electronic report on the PDA and send this off to the office. Now, off to the next call!

Every visit is similar but different as you need to keep your wits about you to ensure that you do not miss anything as it is so important to be accurate.

The thing with auditing is every store's layout and ranges can differ so you have to make sure you walk all the way round the store a few times.

Some people may think it must be a bit repetitive – but not me, I love it!

Auditing offers different takes on the same data

The data collected during an audit can be analysed from different angles, by a variety of products, by product variant, by store type, by distribution channel, by region and so on. Improvements in the outlets over a series of visits can be measured in different ways too.

For example, the positioning of each product can be varied so that the most effective method of promotion and sale are developed. Did the placing on a shelf improve if it was on a higher or a lower shelf? Does it matter in the outlet where the product is located? The answer is it does matter.

Underhill (2003) describes research where they tested different locations, for example for sales of Aspirin. Older people, the main purchasers of Aspirin, bought less if Aspirin was located near teenage products such as cold drinks. They bought more if it was located at the right height and in a logical place as perceived by the older buyer.

Auditing in practice

Auditing is the use of the field personnel to gather meaningful information about the distribution of products, services or point of sale. This will involve data capture and analysis, usually with a personal digital assistant (PDA) or laptop, with results often available on the web in real time (see Chapter 11).

The types of data collected vary, but might include any of the following:

- store size (for potential secondary displays, extra sales);
- store location (to plan activities targeted to location, for example near schools or a city centre);
- store status (independent, symbol group or multiple – because they all operate in different ways);
- number of products stocked, sizes or varieties (client products, so that further products can be sold in, and for future calls to measure any improvement);
- number of facings per product or size and placing of products (this assesses if the product has sufficient shelf space and visibility);
- prices (to check whether these are correct);
- competitor range and prices (to assess what the competitors are achieving);
- delivery days (to know the best days to call and take orders, and the best day to avoid calling as the store will be busy with a delivery and have no time to stop);
- local cash and carry used or other distribution channel (so that selling in can be planned, and stock availability checked at those distribution channels);
- usual order sizes (to evaluate whether they are ordering enough stock).

There will be many more elements, depending on the product and/or the exercise.

The audits could be conducted:

- by product;
- by a named store group or to independents;

- by region, by area manager or by TV area;
- by footprint for a particular distribution centre, for example cash and carry or warehouse;
- nationally for many store groups or independent outlets;
- focused on target demographics, for example age, gender or profession.

In a large supermarket it is very difficult for the store to check on the vast array of products displayed. The following case study shows how FM ambassadors focusing on their clients' range of products can assist the store in this checking, and thus help prevent the errors that are bound to occur. In this case study the FM ambassadors assist the store and the client by reducing errors in the first instance and then offering ongoing prevention, which enables the product to be on shelf, correctly labelled and ready for sale.

Case study: Book stock errors and shelf edge labels

Chapter 5 explained two in-store items that would be checked by compliance – book stock errors (BSE) and shelf edge labels (SEL).

BSEs are when the book in-store states that the product is in stock, when in fact it is out of stock in the warehouse. Of course, this will definitely affect sales as the product will run out on the shelves and as there is no stock held, there will be a wait until the new stock comes in

SELs are important, as without them the customer does not know the correct price of the product, and this will deter them from purchasing.

Taking just these two points, an audit was commenced.

Process

The results from the previous four months were charted, when there were no visits from FM staff to assist with identifying and correcting any faults, and these were used as a measure for improvement once the FM visits began.

The change was charted through 10 months of consistent visits, and the very damaging BSEs were reduced dramatically, which is a huge support to the store, but also to the supplier.

SELs are not helped by people walking up and down the aisles and moving and touching them, but even so there was a significant improvement.

The effect is shown in Figure 6.1.

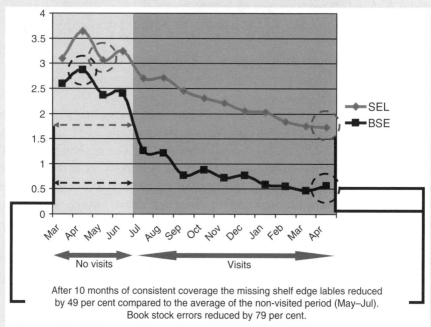

After 10 months of consistent coverage the missing shelf edge lables reduced by 49 per cent compared to the average of the non-visited period (May–Jul). Book stock errors reduced by 79 per cent.

Figure 6.1 BSE and SEL

Results

Immediately as the staff started to visit the store, the problems with SELs fell by 33 per cent and the BSEs by 66 per cent, and over a continuous time this improved to a reduction of 49 per cent on problems with SELs and 79 per cent on BSEs. At its worst there were 3.7 SELs missing and 2.8 BSEs as an average per store, and this was reduced at the end of the 10 months to an average of 1.7 SELs missing and 0.5 BSEs.

The significance of this is that the products were correctly marked with the SELs making purchasing easier. The BSEs being rectified meant that the product was much less likely to be found out of stock.

This is important because if the product is not there, it cannot be bought, and incorrect labelling might also cause a reduction in sales.

Auditing figures and gaining results like those shown in the above case study show us that it is very important to track the sales fundamentals, as these will have a direct implication on the sales of a brand.

As for merchandising and auditing, the old maxim applies, if it is not there or it cannot be seen, then it cannot be purchased and sales are lost. In the following case study the extreme consequences of not doing an audit are clear.

Case study: Fast-moving consumer goods (FMCG)

Background

The background was that a new product variant had been developed, at a very significant cost by a large supplier of several 'must stock' lines to the grocery trade. A major multiple retailer had listed the product in **all** outlets for a trial period.

The problem

One Friday night, with the trial period ended and a meeting with the buyer for the grocery multiple scheduled for the following Tuesday, the sales director rang to discuss why the sales of the product were so far short of expectations. Working through the possible errors, the conclusion was that perhaps all the stores had not carried the product, and thus the sales were not as expected, and this needed to be checked. Last thing on the Friday night a nationwide call went out to auditors round the country and asked them to visit some of the outlets and to confirm on Monday the name and address of the outlet and whether the product was stocked. A report was received from about 300 outlets, which was an excellent sample size. On Monday night the result was faxed to the sales director at his hotel. A full report showing that of the sample visited, the product was only stocked in 34 per cent of the stores.

Result

The next morning, the buyer was expecting, on the sales performance, to de-list the product, thus wasting all the development costs. However, the report was presented, the product had a second chance, and now many years later it is a 'must stock' item in any grocery multiple in the UK.

Not all audits have such a quantifiable dramatic effect as seen in the FMCG case study, but with distribution and availability being so crucial to the sales process, it is always prudent to know where your product is, and in what quantity!

Tips for planning an audit

The critical points for a successful audit are:

- Check where the visits need to be made, and select the call file carefully, so that the exercise will deliver exactly what the client needs. Check the integrity of the call file.

- Ensure that the content of the call is clear. The auditors should know exactly what they are looking for, what they need to record, questions they should ask, and data they should capture.
- If the data is to be captured by PDA or other data capture tools (see Chapter 11) and the captured data is relayed to the web, a system needs to be in place for ongoing analysis, so that the data is used to trigger swift corrective action if it is necessary.
- Ensure that the PDAs are configured for all the information that is required, and listen to suggestions from the FM company, as FM personnel will have experience of what information can be most useful, according to the objectives of the exercise. Some information might well add significant value to the exercise.
- Train the staff so that they know exactly what is expected of them, and exactly what the client wishes to achieve, as this will assist in a proper delivery of the campaign.
- Analyse the data to see what can be learned, and whether the data highlights any weaknesses that can be improved upon or strengths that can be developed. If more calls are to be made to the same or similar outlets, then the development of brand availability and distribution can be tracked, and linked to the sales data; the importance of the sales fundamentals will be proven.

Summary

Auditing is the FM element of the face-to-face mix that reports on how a brand and its competitors are distributed, both across stores and in-store and how it is displayed in terms of facings and placings, stock levels, the management of the stock, order sizes, etc. This allows decisions to be made on the need for other FM disciplines or other marketing activities to support the brand. Audits and analysis of the data acquired can now be carried out in near real-time through improved technology and communication capability.

Self-study questions

6.1. Name two of the most common reasons for conducting an audit.
6.2. What is a book stock error, and why is it important that they are kept to a minimum?
6.3. Why might you need to capture data on store size and store location?

(Answers can be found in the text.)

7 The FM sampling and demonstrating discipline

Sampling and demonstrating as an FM discipline are always face to face; that is, in the presence of an FM staff member, who guides the customer through the sampling or demonstrating process and notes any customer reaction and responds to it. Sampling is straightforward and often is a simple taste or smell opportunity, whereas demonstrating can be a more complex exercise where the consumer is shown how a product operates. While carrying out sampling or demonstrating, the FM staff will be communicating – describing the product or service, its features and benefits while informing and educating the listener. The FM staff person is the brand ambassador. A key difference between sampling and experiential marketing is that the latter uses the five senses to involve the customer, who is frequently a hands-on participant.

Conducting a sampling or demonstration activity should not be taken lightly, there are many rules. There are many positives too, as the consumers become aware of the brand and its attributes, and this will aid the sales drive considerably.

Definitions

Sampling is when the consumer is offered the opportunity to try a product in the presence of an FM person who explains, influences and presents the product in a positive light, often by focusing on taste or smell of a product.

Food and drink, perfumes and aftershaves fit this sampling category. Samples may be handed out for later consumption, such as shampoos, newspapers, printed materials or software on disk. There is a crossover with sampling and experiential marketing (see Chapter 8).

Demonstrating is when the product or service is shown, explained and demonstrated, to consumers: the consumer observes and sometimes operates the product as demonstrated. These are typically demonstrations of small domestic items related to the kitchen or for cleaning the house, or mobile phones and other technology.

The value is that people who have sampled or been demonstrated to now 'understand' the product. People will always talk about a product and use it when they understand it, and feel comfortable with it.

Sampling

As outlined above, sampling is the use of field personnel to present potential users with a product or service. It is an important part of brand awareness, as it allows the consumer to trial the product or service. This could apply to a variety of products from a chocolate bar, a cup of coffee, a shampoo, a newspaper – and with 85 per cent of the business in the UK coming from the service rather than the manufacturing base, many services also use sampling as an effective means of trial; for example, companies providing internet services and mobile phones.

The brand ambassadors will introduce the product to the customer by giving or showing them the sample, explain the benefits of the product and its unique selling points (USPs), offer trials and raise brand visibility. During the sampling a short brand message can be delivered, and a leaflet can accompany samples where appropriate. The more memorable, lively and involving the activity is that surrounds the trial, the better the product recall, and the greater the affinity between the consumer and the brand (see also Chapter 8).

By sampling the product, end users are not only made aware of the product, but they also know that they like it. They have a knowledge of that product, and this understanding will translate into future purchases.

Safety of samples

When offering samples extreme care should be taken to ensure that the safety of the public is paramount in the planning and training stages. For example, should a product contain nuts, this should be explained to the potential consumer before they trial the product in case they have an allergy.

Similarly, children should never be given sweets unless a responsible adult agrees, as the child could be diabetic or forbidden to speak to strangers. These are obvious examples, but some dangers are less so. Your FM partner will advise you on this. (See also the 'Guide to responsible sampling' available from the DMA website: www.dma.org.uk).

Presentation of samples

Products should always be presented in prime condition so that, with a food or drink product, it tastes its best, and this can cause extra logistical issues at the point of sampling. For example, sampling a soft drink on a railway station concourse will require many large fridges on the concourse to keep the drink cold, so that it tastes its best. Heating a product must be done carefully to the correct temperature, so ovens and microwaves will need to be used.

Health and safety

Products must always be presented safely too. Food items that must be kept chilled, must also be kept chilled at a sampling event by law. For example, ice cream samples at a county show must be in a freezer van so that the dairy product will not deteriorate and cause a health problem. The temperature must be maintained in the van too, so there must be regular trips to run the engine of the van to run the cooling units. There could well be a visit from the health and safety people to check the van.

When working with food products and preparing them for sampling, the staff must all have a hygiene certificate and must also be supplied with the equipment to keep their workstation clean. This may include (depending on the product being sampled) disposable plates, knives, cups and hygienic wipes for the surfaces.

Environmental hazard

Significant care should be taken to ensure that the personnel are present at the venue legally and where leaflets are involved ensure that FM staff clear up if people drop them (dropped leaflets could be a fire hazard as well as being offensive in that they are creating an environmental mess). Some councils now require that organizations hold a licence for handing out leaflets. The Clean Neighbourhoods Environment Act 2005 is now becoming more well known, and is enforced more frequently. This Act restricts the areas where leaflets can be distributed, and both the FM company and the client could be fined if they are incorrectly located. The only exemptions are for charity, religion and politics. It is the act of distributing the leaflets that is the offence, not the litter created by the act. An FM company will advise on this and other restrictions that apply depending on where the work is to be conducted.

Equipment safety

If equipment is used to assist the sampling activity; for example, stands, cooking implements, lighting, etc then these must all be safe and checked. For example, a stand placed in a public place must be made of fire retardant materials in order to meet fire regulations, and there must not be trailing electrical leads or wire that could trip someone up.

Couponing

To encourage future purchase, money-off coupons can be distributed with the sample, and the monitored redemption of the coupons is an excellent way of measuring the response to an activity. Of course, people will be pleased to have the opportunity to sample a product, and the activity will have generated awareness, but awareness cannot be easily quantified in terms of ROI whereas coupon redemption can (see Cummins and Mullin, 2008, *Sales Promotion*, Kogan Page, and the Voucher Association website). There is also a new technique developing in 2007 known as 'SMS couponing' which is relevant.

Demonstrating

Potential customers often find making choices about product type or service difficult, as they do not know all the features and benefits. Once these are explained, their choices are easier, and good demonstrations will lead to increased sales. The FM person is the brand ambassador.

Based in high customer traffic areas where the target consumers are passing, FM staff members demonstrate the features and benefits of a new or existing product in order to increase product awareness and stimulate purchase. The products could be anything from coffee machines, food processors or vegetable choppers to carpet cleaners or vacuum cleaners. Anyone who has ever been to exhibitions such as the Ideal Home Exhibition knows exactly what demonstrating to gain sales means. Services can be demonstrated too; for example, internet access, mobile telephones, computer software, etc.

Indoors and outdoors

Sampling and demonstrating in-store

There are some restrictions on in-store sampling. For example, there may be limited space, some stores have fixed agreements with specific agencies for the work in their outlets and some staff in these stores may not reflect the brand. Working in-store, however, offers a closeness to the point of purchase and can be highly influential.

When next you go into a supermarket and there is a stand where you can try a product; that is sampling. Next time you see a promotion like this, stop and watch for a few minutes, and you will see many of the items we have discussed – disposable implements, hygienic wipes for the surfaces, an explanation of the product and so on.

Sampling and demonstrating outdoors

Here there is the advantage to work and engage the customer without blocking the aisles, so there is an opportunity to make the promotion bigger, with increased branding and a professional set, for example a trailer. Using a big trailer allows the promotion to move maximizing the value from the budget (county shows, employee events, car park activities). Outdoor events offer fewer constraints on staffing, as people can be recruited who reflect the brand and are very knowledgeable about it.

Case study: A day in the life of a demonstrator

After practising all week since the training course with the food processor I feel confident now and last night went to the supermarket to buy the items on the shopping list supplied at the training.

7.30 am – Leave the house (my husband scraped the ice off the windscreen) and drive to the department store where I shall be working for the next three days.

8.15 am – Park up and arrive at the store. Check in with security. I am given a badge and directed to the kitchen department. It's a lot to carry so I am glad I borrowed my Mum's shopping trolley.

8.30 am – Arrive in the kitchen department – nobody here. I don't like to set up without knowing exactly where they want me.

8.40 am – Supervisor for kitchens arrives and suggests a spot at the back; not a good place at all, so I choose a better spot nearer the main traffic areas and she agrees.

8.45 am – I cleared the demonstration table of a small display and put these items in a box in the stockroom. I set up my demo processor with all the gadgets displayed. I put some ingredients out and put the rest under the demonstration table as they do have to last all day. I find the kitchenette where I can wash the gadgets, and I have my own tea towel so I'm ready.

9.10 am – The area looks very tidy and now I must wait for the customers. With the build up to Christmas I am sure the processors will make good presents. Mental note to speak to men too as they may purchase for women.

2.00 pm – Just had lunch and I've sold three processors so far – not too bad for a first day.

4.00 pm – I would like it to be busier. I am worried about stocks, so the supervisor has called more up from the warehouse. That should sort me out for tomorrow, then we can get another uplift tomorrow afternoon ready for Saturday. Knowing I was coming, they increased their order and there are in total (shop and warehouse) 25 processors in stock, I hope that's enough. It has slowed down in the kitchen department. I have only sold one more (24 left). The kitchen supervisor is very impressed – they didn't sell one last week.

5.30 pm – Wash up, tidy up and leave everything ready for tomorrow.

I'm changing my hours for tomorrow, starting later – working 10.30 through to 6.30 to catch more shoppers.

5.50 pm – Sign out at security. Drive home via the supermarket for the ingredients for tomorrow and Saturday.

7.05 pm – Home!

Footnote: Linda worked the next two days (Friday and Saturday). She left the store at 4.00 pm on Saturday when she had sold all the stock.

Important points

Here are some important points to consider when sampling or demonstrating:

- The staff need to be well trained and fully conversant with the item to be sampled or demonstrated.
- If the product to be sampled is a food product, then health and safety laws apply, and the FM staff need to hold a food hygiene certificate, and the surfaces on which they work need to be appropriate for the product. The equipment must be kept clean according to the health and safety rules. The sampler will also need equipment for safe sampling as previously described.
- The environment needs to be conducive to inviting people to participate, and also needs to be visible to attract attention. Thought must be given to stands, uniforms, equipment and any other ancillary items that might be needed to enhance the activity and make the approach a comfortable one for the consumer.
- All the ancillary items must meet health and safety standards, and must also meet local rules that might apply; for example, most shopping centres will not allow a stand to be more than 6 feet tall. If a motor vehicle is to be shown in an indoor environment, then the vehicle must contain no petrol or oil so that it is not a potential fire hazard. A professional FM company will be able to advise and deal with these and other relevant issues.
- Insurances must be in place and must be shown to the owner of the promotional location. Public liability is usually required for £10 million or more, staff should be insured in the workplace and professional indemnity insurance is also requested from time to time (see Chapter 17).
- Legal placing of the activity is important. Permission should be sought (and paid for) so that the brand is not seen to be breaking any rules. This point may not apply to guerrilla or bandit activity where the brand profile is 'edgy' or 'naughty' and where the surprise and unexpected approach fits the brand (see Chapter 8).

Case study: Sampling

Objective

Product launch for new confectionery product, with the aim to sample as many people as possible.

Activity

In support of extensive TV, press and radio advertisements 1,000 FM brand ambassadors were placed in one TV region on one day.

Staff were in many retail outlets, amusement areas, shopping centres, cinemas, with uniforms, character costumes, stands and over 1 million samples.

Results

In one day in one TV region over 1 million samples were distributed of this new product. The activity was rolled out TV region by TV region. The product is now a must stock item in any outlet anywhere that sells confectionery.

The huge visibility for the product in the TV region was remarkable, and it made the local press and local TV news too. Superb visibility for the brand.

Case study: Demonstration

Objective

To introduce business people to a clients' online banking service that offers particular advantages to businesses. The system also offers advantages to the user for personal banking.

Activity

A fully trained demonstrator was placed in the departure lounge of terminal 1 at Heathrow, where the business community were catching planes. The stand was set up with laptops and a fully interactive system so that the website could be accessed and demonstrated. Every passenger who received a demonstration was given a cup of coffee in return for their business card.

Results

Many passengers received the presentation and were happy to leave their business cards in exchange for a cup of coffee. The business cards were then used as a telesales tool to contact the travellers to promote the product, and to sell to their businesses or to themselves personally.

This activity was repeated several times, as the quality of the leads was excellent and sales resulted.

Summary

The FM sampling and demonstrating discipline allows the customer to have a dialogue with a brand ambassador while trialling or observing a product or service. This matches the customers' need in 2007 to obtain brand experience and develop a relationship with the brand. There are health and safety risks, legal and insurance implications and other hazards of which account has to be taken when setting up sampling or demonstrating.

Self-study questions

7.1. When food sampling what should you consider?
7.2. What is the benefit of using coupons with sampling?
7.3. What precautions have be taken with a car being shown indoors?

(Answers can be found in the text.)

8 The FM experiential marketing, roadshows and events discipline

It was Confucius who said, 'Tell me and I will hear, show me and I will see, involve me and I will believe'. In the past few years there has been more involvement of the audience by the introduction of theatre and creativity to gain the audience's buy-in to the brand through emotional and sensory involvement. This has become known as live brand experience or experiential marketing. Although this FM discipline is not new, it is an interactive development of the events discipline and it is becoming increasingly recognized as more companies choose to specialize in it.

Definitions

The Experiential Marketing Committee (part of the DMA) has stated that: 'Experiential marketing is a live and interactive marketing discipline, which builds positive emotional sensory engagement between a brand and its consumers.'

A roadshow is when a promotional activity is created, which then moves around the country, for example when a radio station has promotional trips to different seaside resorts in the summer. An event is an activity that does not move. This might be promotional activity in a shopping centre, at an exhibition, in a car park or at a county show for example, although of course events can be conducted at more than one venue across the country, thus the difference between a roadshow and an event is blurred.

Roadshows and events can be truly experiential when they appeal to the consumer's senses and involve them in the brand and the activity.

Experiential marketing, roadshows and events are designed to meet the consumers of the brand in question, and through trial, sampling and interactive involvement to develop an affinity with the brand, which will generate positive awareness and drive sales.

A day in the life of an experiential marketing field ambassador

8.30 am – I start early by making pre-visit calls to the pubs – 10 in total, just to make sure that the managers are there at the arranged times. It's going to be a busy day/night trying to take 600 students around 10 pubs/clubs while at the same time promoting the product!

9.15 am – Check that I have all the relevant POS, samples, etc for the day's/night's activities, which are going to be huge!

9.20 am – Run through and journey plan my list of calls for the day.

9.30 am – Leave the house ready for the day's/night's activities.

10.30 am – Arrive at the first call. Check the outlet has been fully merchandized and try and negotiate with the manager maximum top shelf space for the brand. I need to make sure that the staff have all their uniforms and that they are aware of the activity. If none of them have tried the product before I will give them a couple of samples to try. The rest of the day carries on in much the same format. I need to make sure I visit all 10 outlets that are taking part in the pub crawl.

4.30 pm – I have just finished my last call and have just enough time to grab something to eat before I meet up with the student pub crawl team.

5.00 pm – Meet up with the student samplers in our first watering hole to arrange the route. We will need to make sure that the 600-strong group visit the same pubs but at different times as a result of the fantastic response to the event. Due to the number of students who will be taking part in the pub crawl we will need to split up into seven teams, with each team consisting of 80 people.

7.00 pm	– Students start to arrive at the venue, and everyone seems very excited. I can't wait to get going – it will be a fantastic opportunity to gain publicity for the brand.
7.30 pm	– After trying to gain some control over the 500 and something students (after the last count!) each team heads off at 10-minute intervals.
2.00 am	– (next day!) Finally able to leave the lively bunch to head off to bed. Tonight has been a great success with lots of positive feedback on the brand. I think I will wait until tomorrow now to type up and send back my report!

Purpose

The purpose of experiential marketing, roadshows and events is to generate brand awareness and brand loyalty in a lively and engaging manner that reflects the brand image and values, and it is an entertaining way of putting a product or service in the public eye.

Part of the development of this brand awareness is to engage the public with the product by running an event or a roadshow. This can also be a lively part of any integrated campaign, and events are becoming one of the key methods of attracting the consumer to participate with the brand and associate it with enjoyment, and through this pleasurable experience, develop an affinity with the brand that will lead to purchase.

Interestingly, many venues that have been used for years by field marketers are now actively looking for interactive, lively activity on their premises. They wish to see their visitors entertained (and not hassled) as part of the pleasurable experience in the venue, for example at a shopping centre.

This discipline involves putting on a show that involves the product and the potential consumers, so that the sampling of the product is an experience for the consumer, who has an opportunity to interact with the product, have fun and thus develop an identity with the brand.

Experiential marketing at its best is a very creative event that will reflect the brand being experienced. It is creative in every sense of the word – in conception, visually, emotionally and in its execution. It is designed to win the hearts and minds of consumers and to get them to develop an involvement with the brand.

Obviously a balance has to be found between the impact and excitement of the activity and the logistics and safety aspects that must be in place before it goes live.

Location, location – the venue

Where to hold the event

Whether the event is termed a roadshow or a live brand experience, it must be held where the target consumer market is prolific, so that there are many positive experiences, for example events held at music festivals and rock concerts will target young people, events at popular seaside resorts are held to meet families, events on railway concourses target commuters.

Many FM companies have offered this discipline for years, have exciting experiential work to their credit, and often use this as a part of an integrated campaign. Once all the distribution and stocking issues are in place, these events come into their own, as they will maximize the pull-through of product from the stores in the locality of the event.

There are times when the experience is not specifically related to the product, but reflects the product, or encourages the consumer to be in the frame of mind to accept the product easily. For example, when sampling a beauty magazine, the offer of a massage, a makeover, a pedicure or some other beauty treatment on the stand, prior to being given a copy of the magazine, makes the moment of being asked to take and read the magazine memorable, and the attitude to the experience, and thus the magazine, will be positive.

For a deodorant or aftershave targeted at sporty action men, the activity could be linked to a sporting event. Even on a stand they could kick goals, drive cars round a track (electronically), bowl a cricket ball or take a golf shot. This activity conducted in front of their peers will be memorable, and if the experience is a good one for them and one at which they have fun, then the brand will be readily recalled and this will lead to purchase.

Be aware that organizing experiential work, events and roadshows is a specialist task, and you will need a company that can do the work, so that you are sure you are covered in terms of complete delivery and for health and safety and legalities.

Venues

There are several different types of venue where these activities can take place:

- In-store. There may be limitations with space as activities could block the customer traffic.

- Concourse – for example railway stations, shopping centres where space has to be booked and paid for, usually fairly spacious.
- Exhibition – either on an exhibition stand, in the foyer or even outside the venue.
- Outdoors – for example at a rock concert, by the beach, at a county show, in a large recreation area or in the street. Sites will need to be booked and paid for. Outdoor events are often subject to weather issues and are often seasonal or cyclical.

Case study: digital TV sales

Background

The football season starts in August and every year a digital TV sports channel increases its coverage on Premiership League games. During the season this channel will show a large number of live football games and a minimum of 50 minutes of each premiership match.

Objectives

To promote the benefit of the subscription to customers, enabling them to 'watch their own team at home'.

Execution

Ten Comet stores were visited for 6 days in August (60 store visits in total). There were three FDS staff members present in each store on each date. One FDS staff member was product trained and that person's main role was to demonstrate the benefits and functions of an enhanced TV package. The two remaining FDS staff were responsible for setting up football games and interacting with customers so that customers wanted to play the games. For example, a goal area was set up in each car park that gave customers the chance to win prizes such as towels and T-shirts. FDS staff encouraged customers to go into the store and to receive a demonstration of the product.

Results

This activity was very successful as it generated a total of 118 sales of product. On average 19.6 sales were made per day of the activity. During the whole activity 3,555 customers were spoken to and one out of every three customers wanted to receive a demonstration.

Guerrilla activity

There is one type of activity where site fees do not apply, and that is the area of guerrilla or bandit sampling.

This is the only area where permission is not usually sought, which is fine, providing the client is prepared for the occasional complaint. Complaints are usually few and far between, as the activity is only in one place for a very short space of time. Usually the team will drive up, stop, jump out of the vehicle, deliver samples or the brand message to those present, and then leave as quickly and unexpectedly as they arrived. If challenged, they apologize profusely and depart immediately. Particular care must be taken with guerrilla activity, and in-depth training on the modus operandi is crucial so that as many problems are planned out as possible. This is also an area where the management must be strong and plentiful, so that issues can be dealt with at once. The element of surprise is very much a part of the guerrilla activity, it is quick and fun, but must be scrupulously trained and planned.

Booking

Legal and proper placement of activities

As stated in Chapter 7, and again above, the sites to be visited for activities must be attended lawfully. This does involve booking the sites, paying fees and carrying extensive insurance.

An FM company will assist with the booking and will know the best sites to visit. There are also agencies who will locate and book sites.

There are a few points to bear in mind:

- The best venues are booked up well in advance – some shopping centres, for example, can be booked up to a year ahead.
- Shopping centres in particular may not take activities in during November and December when the promotional sites are used by Christmas trees, decorations and Santa's grotto.
- The venues are able to make extra revenue from charging for the space, and the cost of some of the venues is very high.
- Outdoor events may well be subject to weather issues.

Case study: Sunsilk sampling campaign

In support of the launch of Lever Fabergé's 'Sunsilk Frizz Control Cream', their below-the-line agency, KLP Euro RSCG, devised a campaign, calling upon FDS to recruit, train and manage the field personnel. The task was to deploy profiled teams on branded scooters across the UK to distribute 1 million product samples in 20 days, a challenge FDS gladly accepted.

Before any fieldwork could start FDS held castings, together with our client, to recruit three teams of Sunsilk brand ambassadors. Each person was handpicked to ensure that they were representative of the brand, a 'frizz-free' head of hair was a necessity!

Our next mission involved guiding half our team members through two motor-bike tests. Initially they had to pass their compulsory basic training before pro-gressing to the full motorbike test, to enable passengers to be carried and a trailer to be towed. This was not the easiest task to complete, but FDS rose to the challenge and enough riders were suitably qualified for the start of the campaign.

Our roving teams visited 35 towns across the country. The image of eight females arriving in town centres on four branded scooters and trailers turned a few heads! But just to ensure that everyone in the vicinity was aware of their presence, weather-oriented music was played, to drive home the key insight behind the brand.

The promotion definitely had the desired effect. Half a million pillow-packs were distributed, each containing two samples of the frizz control cream, a leaflet to highlight the key product benefits and details of a free prize draw. As a result, excellent brand recognition and awareness from passing consumers was achieved. The core brand values were reinforced in conjunction with the above-the-line campaign.

Issues arising from the Sunsilk case study

This example is selected as there are some very obvious, and potentially very serious, issues with this roadshow.

Here are a few of them:

- There was a significant challenge in recruiting carefully profiled staff who were prepared to take their motorbike tests – and not all of them passed.
- The scooters and the trailers had to be branded.
- Scooters and all the stock of pillow packs needed to be transported safely to the cities in which they were to work.
- Contingency was needed if a scooter broke down.

- Insurance had to be in place in case of an accident.
- Permission to visit the cities had to be gained.
- Planning was needed on where to meet at each city to avoid causing a nuisance when the scooters were unloaded.
- Staff had to be moved around the country to conduct the activity in the different cities.
- Safety was paramount, so staff had to be careful where they parked their scooters when they stopped to distribute the samples and deliver the brand messages to passers-by.
- And on top of all this were the requirements for staff training on product knowledge, the logistics of the operation and also extensive contingency 'What if ...?' planning and instruction.

To conduct an exercise such as this without the knowledge and support of a professional FM company would be very unwise, and could cause significant brand damage if anything went wrong.

Assessing the results

Results from experiential, roadshow or event work

The measurement of results in this type of face-to-face marketing can be more difficult than for other disciplines within the FM spectrum. As you will have read, the results for sales and merchandising, for example, can be measured so precisely, that the benefit to the bottom line can be measured and quantified.

With experiential marketing the results are often less easy to define. In the case study above, we know that 1 million women who suffer from frizzy hair in certain weather conditions were very accurately targeted and given a free sample of a hair product, but in this campaign there was no requirement to measuring the exact pull-through on sales that this generated, although through the prize draw names and addresses were collected as a permission marketing tool for future contact with consumers.

Undoubtedly the activity generated a huge amount of visibility and awareness for the brand, but awareness cannot always be quantified. There is nothing wrong with stating that awareness and recognition are the main objectives and results – after all the advertising industry cover this all the time – but should a client want to be able to quantify the effect of work conducted in the field, then experiential work might not be the best route for that client to take. (See Chapter 14, where there is a suggested ROI model for sampling.)

There are ways of quantifying the sales made from sampling in some exercises, where the activity is in a well-defined area, for example in the footprint of a specific store, and here an uplift in sales can be monitored. If money-off coupons are distributed, the redemption of these can be analysed too.

Summary

The words lively, fun, engaging, and entertaining describe what should be different about this FM discipline. It offers the customer the opportunity to experience the brand in a way that allows the chance to find out how the customer might behave with the brand. The customer can experience the senses generated by the brand and start to build an emotional relationship. As for sampling and demonstrating, this matches customers' needs in 2007 to obtain brand experience and develop a relationship with the brand. Again there are health and safety risks, legal and insurance implications and other hazards of which account has to be taken when setting up experiential marketing, roadshows and events.

Self-study questions

8.1. What is experiential marketing? What is the difference between a roadshow and an event?
8.2. What is the purpose of this FM discipline?
8.3. What has to be considered in a venue?

(Answers can be found in the text.)

9 The FM mystery calling and shopping discipline

Used as a tool to check the standards, generally in the service industry, mystery shopping is when highly trained FM staff, posing as customers, are sent to a venue to assess it against strict preset criteria.

Mystery calling can be exactly the same thing, and the names are frequently used synonymously. However, mystery calling is also a term that is used when mystery telephone calls are made.

Though some might believe that this discipline is just a concealed form of auditing, it is quite different and recognized as such by the FMC. Auditing does not examine the performance of people but the physical reality. Mystery calling and shopping test the operation of staff to confirm training standards and service delivery at the face-to-face point. In that respect mystery calling and shopping has a tendency towards the subjective and great efforts are taken to make it as objective an activity as possible.

There are two types of mystery visit:

- covert – when the person making the visit does not let anyone know they are there from beginning to the end of the call;
- overt – when the mystery visit is conducted, but at the very end of the call the mystery person reveals to the outlet that they are there.

Definitions

Mystery shopping and mystery calling – (in the FM industry the discipline is commonly given either name) – is a covert face-to-face approach in which a trained mystery shopper will visit an outlet to make assessments.

Examples of mystery shopping

- Visit a retail outlet to check on the sales assistant's product knowledge.
- Stay in a hotel to assess the service.
- Eat in a restaurant to sample the food and service.
- Visit a pub to ensure that a drink is correctly presented.
- Visit a car showroom for a test drive.
- Visit or call on professional institutions staff.

Purpose of mystery shopping

The purpose of the mystery visit is to:

- check the quality and standards within the outlet visited;
- reward good practice from outlet staff;
- uncover training needs within the outlet.

Background

To maximize the sales effort for any product or service, the brand manager must be sure that the product or service is available and well received at the point of purchase. To achieve this, the brand manager may, for example, have invested in the outlets and implemented extensive training, introduced new systems, new standards of customer care, developed service standards and implemented quality checks.

Having made this investment, the brand manager needs to measure the effectiveness of these initiatives and see how they operate after implementation, and to do this the manager uses mystery shopping.

Assessing the standards

Mystery shoppers are carefully trained so that they fully understand what they should expect to experience when they visit the outlet. It is important that the training is very clear, as the results of the call must be as objective as possible so that the outlet is measured against what the client wishes to be happening, and not a subjective view of the mystery shopper. A comprehensive report form will be completed and this will also help the mystery shopper to keep to the objective view as much as possible.

A mystery shopper will then visit the outlet posing as a customer and during the visit will assess the outlet against these preset criteria. Once the mystery shopper has left the outlet, he or she will complete the report form, and this will be sent off for analysis and reporting to the client.

If the call is an 'overt' call, then the mystery shopper will tell the outlet who he or she is, but only at the end of the call, after the assessment has been completed. Most often this reveal is to reward good practice in the outlet, and to thank the outlet for good performance on behalf of the client. However, there are times when the reveal is to explain that the mystery call was not successful and the mystery shopper must then explain why the experience was not a good one, and will often conduct some retraining in store at the time of the visit or make an appointment for a further visit for corrective action.

For example, when in a pub the drink in question is correctly presented, the landlord is congratulated and offered a gift. Where it is not correctly presented, the mystery shopper will leave without telling the publican he or she was there, and report back to the client. The area manager will then visit the pub to train the staff again.

Excerpt from a day in the life of a mystery shopper

Background

A manufacturer of computers had launched a new printer. The managers in computer shops had been trained to the features and benefits of the printer, and had been charged with training their staff to these features and benefits. The managers were given posters and printed information to put up in their staffrooms and to use at a training session.

Two weeks later the managers were sent an incentive, and they were told that there would be a night out for all their staff if they pass a few product knowledge challenges, including three mystery shopping visits. A chart was sent to the manager to be put up in the staffroom, and every time a challenge was passed (either a telephone challenge, the client area manager challenge or one of the three mystery shopping challenges) they would be given a sticker to put on their chart. If they filled the chart with stickers, they won their night out.

The Day

Today I am off to visit computer shops, which is interesting as I am not very technical. I have to go in and ask for a printer 'for my husband', I have to make a few statements of what he is looking for (which I have practised) and I must listen to their responses. They gain points if they mention the particular printer I am mystery shopping, and gain points for every one of the features and benefits they tell me.

8.15 – Leave the house and drive to the first store. I went in and wandered around the printer display. A young man, Alan, came and talked to me, and I explained that I was researching for a printer for my husband. I told him what PC my husband had, and explained the sort of thing my husband wanted, according to the brief.

He explained a competitor printer to me (but maybe that was because it was quite close to where we were standing). I listened and asked him if there were others that might also be suitable. The third printer he showed me was the client's printer. He told me all about it, gave me some literature, and I left the shop.

Back in the car I took out the report form. I marked off the features and benefits that Alan had given me about the client's printer against a preset report form, and added up the points. I am only allowed to offer a sticker if they reach a certain level of points.

He did! I then went back into the store, and found Alan. I asked him to take me to the manager, at which point he looked very scared! I reassured him that it was 'something nice'. We met the manager and I explained that I had been very happy with the help that Alan had given me, and that Alan had won the store a sticker for their chart. I was taken into the staffroom and allowed to see the chart. There were a couple of people in there, who were very pleased to see a sticker go up!

9.40 – I thanked Alan and the manager, and went on my way to the next call.

Mystery shopping as a development tool

It is also possible to make a series of mystery visits to the same outlets over a period of time. The results of the first visit are fed back to the outlet, then the second visit (say three months later) will assess if the lessons from the first call have been learned. Of course, for this type of exercise to retain the mystery element, the mystery shopper must be a different person from visit to visit so that he or she is not spotted. In this scenario the mystery shopping is used not only to check the standards and quality, but also becomes a development tool.

Indeed, the Financial Services Authority (FSA) have very strict rules and codes of conduct for the selling of financial packages, and mystery shopping an FSA salesperson is a very good way of knowing that he or she is behaving ethically, giving the correct information and conducting himself or herself properly. At worst, this mystery exercise could catch a rogue, but that is very rare indeed; most often the worst-case scenario is that a little further training might be highlighted. Obviously, in this scenario the mystery customer has to be very highly trained so that they know what the salesperson is stating incorrectly and correctly.

The mystery shopper's audit

The audit and the training

For a mystery shop to be effective the audit must be as objective as possible and there must be strict rules in place so that the methodology is not ambiguous. The mystery shoppers (if there are more than one) must be carefully trained, so that they are consistent across all venues. The FM company, with the client, will draw up the rules and the checklist, and train the mystery shoppers carefully so that the best results are achieved. It is critical that as much consistency across all outlets to be assessed is as good as it can be, otherwise the outlets themselves might not readily accept the views expressed by the mystery shopper.

Results

The results will show the client the view of the mystery shoppers guided by their training and the objective report form they are assessing each outlet against. These results might show some problems, which can be highlighted and corrected, but will show some successes too, so that staff can be rewarded and congratulated for good practice.

Obviously, the client has 'inside' information that might make an excuse for a particular outlet that has failed a mystery shop. The mystery shopper's views are objective, and in any event present an 'outsider's' view against strict measurement criteria; the view that the customer has too, so even if there are excuses, the value of the mystery call should not be demeaned. If clients find themselves making excuses for outlets, they should be very aware that they have been presented with the view of a member of the public, and should probably question their readiness in making an excuse.

Reporting

Data from the mystery calls can be collected in many different ways (See Chapter 11) and this information collated into a report for the client.

Case study: Mystery motorist campaign

Background

The client is one of the UK providers for conveyor car wash facilities, each site operating as an individual franchise. To improve the professionalism at all outlets the client designed an operator incentive scheme called 'BE: smarter' to assess each franchise on site standards, staff appearance, customer service and sales performance.

Objectives

By deploying mystery motorists across the UK the client would be able to assess current standards at every franchise. All mystery motorists were required to observe various elements at each site including staff appearance, site tidiness and cleanliness and customer service. Points were allocated for each category on which performance could then be judged.

Execution

The activity took place during three phases with three months between each phase. Each phase required the mystery motorists to visit their allocated sites (ie put their car through the car wash) within a four-week period to complete the report forms. Results were sent back to FDS for inputting and at the close of each phase a comprehensive spreadsheet supplied to the client, demonstrating the findings.

Throughout the whole campaign a total of 765 sites were visited.

Results

A slight variation in results was evident between phases with the majority showing positive changes over the three months.

Once viewed by the client all results were forwarded to each individual site, making them aware of any issues, positive or negative.

From these results the client allocated prizes as outlined in the 'BE: smarter' incentive scheme.

Tips for a successful mystery audit

Establish with the client what, in a perfect world, he or she would like to see happening in the outlet. Find out exactly what 'good' looks like, and then with each point try to give guidelines so that the mystery caller can judge in an informed manner. For example: The outside of a pub is to be judged, and one of the questions is 'Is there any litter in the car park?' The guidelines given on this question might be:

- This element is to judge if the landlord or landlady keeps the car park swept and tidy.
- If it is a windy day and a piece of sweet wrapper flies into the car park, but everything else is fine, then you cannot take marks away.
- If however, the fence and the bushes are full of dirty, wet, old litter which looks as though it has been there for weeks then do take marks away.

Spend time and effort making the report form as unambiguous as possible so that answers are largely 'yes' and 'no'. As soon as you ask for the mystery shopper's own view the report will become subjective, unless the mystery shopper has been given detailed guidelines on how to judge the answer to an open question, as detailed in the example in the paragraph above.

This subjective view might be required by the client, and indeed it can be very valuable, but before asking for a shopper's personal view:

- Make sure that they are trained to what the client sees as the correct operation, so that their comments are based on what the client wants to see and whether the client's standards are being met.
- If you have a number of mystery shoppers doing the same task they all need training precisely and exactly to the same brief, otherwise there will be inconsistencies across the different mystery shoppers, and this could highlight inconsistencies across a regional or national spread of outlets.
- Make sure that the mystery shoppers have the image and knowledge to fit the mystery shop in hand, so that they do not stand out as the mystery shopper. For example, send a young person to mystery shop a music store, a more mature person to a restaurant, someone who does not look incongruous in the environment of the mystery shop. The mystery shopper must look like the regular customers.

- Think carefully before you make excuses for an outlet that has been mystery shopped with poor results – the mystery shopper's view will match that of a consumer.

Summary

The discipline of mystery shopping or calling tests the delivery of the product or service to preset criteria. The person carrying out the test must be trained to be as objective as possible and match the expected customer profile. The option to reward in addition to reporting on staff performance is available. The report will state any shortfalls in service or training and may provide incentives for performance, if higher criteria levels are achieved.

Self-study questions

9.1. Give examples of situations which might be mystery shopped.
9.2. What might be the purposes of a mystery visit?
9.3. How does a mystery shopper achieve objectivity?

(Answers can be found in the text.)

10 Ancillaries 1

Training, personnel systems, uniforms, and equipment in the field

By now you will have realized that there is a need for various areas of organizational support for FM, and these are termed ancillary disciplines in this book. In many FM agencies these areas are very skilled indeed.

The topics in the ancillaries have been divided into two chapters and are covered in this chapter and the next one. This chapter covers the people element of support: training, management, their clothing and equipment. (See Chapter 17 for information on the law, including employment law and health and safety.)

Training

Field marketers are adept at training, and this has grown out of their constant need to train their own staff and educate promoters and salespeople about their client's product or service.

In FM, training is conducted at three levels:

- training client customers or customers' personnel, for example in store;
- training field staff for specific exercises, tactical and strategic;
- personnel development within the FM company, for office and field staff.

Training client customers or customer personnel

Any business might require that the people promoting or selling their products need training or retraining. This might be, for example, about a new product, a new system, a new law, or because there needs to be an improvement in the quality of the service offered, as this will aid sales.

A client cannot deal with this internally if there are serious time limits or a large number of outlets to visit. For example, 15,000 retail outlets nationwide where the manager and staff all need training might be covered by an FM company in approximately four weeks, or less if more field people are used, whereas with the limited resource of internal trainers this might take a year or more. The extra sales achieved by instigating the programme speedily will pay for the exercise.

For example, a mobile phone operator was launching a new model of phone, and needed all the retail outlets stocking the phone to understand its features and benefits. This involved visiting 10,000 stores and training the store staff. Due to a level of secrecy, and not wanting the competitors to play any spoiling tactics, the project was kept very quiet. The staff training courses were held up and down the country on a Friday, and the job went live on Monday. All 10,000 stores had to be visited in four days and the training completed by Thursday night, as the extensive and expensive TV advertising campaign was scheduled to commence on Friday night. The public, intrigued by the exciting advertising, would find the product in store on Saturday morning and the in-store staff would be able to demonstrate the phone to them. Eye catching POS material was also placed in each store to add to the awareness.

The alternative of sending written training courses to the outlets direct has yet to be proven worthwhile in FDS' experience, even for the simplest of exercises. The training is either not delivered at all, done at a pace and at a time when it is not effective, or does not include all the relevant people. Field trainers will ensure that they speak to all the staff and the manager, and will ensure that the message is delivered correctly. The field trainer has the delivery of the training as top priority, whereas there will be other priorities for the store manager.

Training field staff for specific exercises, tactical and strategic

Training will precede every single exercise conducted in FM, and this will be by one of the following methods:

- Postal training, where a training document is sent to the staff for them to read. This should be for only the very simplest of activities. FDS as one agency does not often conduct postal briefings as the areas of instruction might be open to misinterpretation, or the priorities of the elements of the task misunderstood.

- Telephone training, where the training document sent is followed up by a telephone call to ensure that the points are all understood, and the emphasis on the thrust of the activity is much more thorough. The telephone call will deal with any of the ambiguities and clarify the priorities.
- Face-to-face training (also called attended training), where all the staff working on a project are collected together with their field managers and trained to the specific task. This might be anything from a half day through to a week or several weeks, depending on the product and the task and their complexity. Face-to-face training of several days is used for the strategic contracts where the ethos of the brand, the project and the details of delivery of the project are complex and must be clearly understood. Longer training sessions also occur for more complex brands, for example insurance products where the FSA rules must also be clear, so that they are adhered to in the field. At an attended briefing the staff can collect the equipment they need for the campaign, so this will save the costs of distributing this to all the staff individually.

The FM company will be able to assist with the decision as to which training would be the best for a programme.

Face-to-face briefings for a national exercise usually occur in three or four cities up and down the country, so that the travelling to each venue is limited and overnight stays do not have to be accommodated in the budget. Although the face-to-face briefings are the most costly, they are also the most effective; and the staff working on the project have the best opportunity to meet the client and learn about the product they are working with first hand. Face-to-face training sessions are worth the investment.

Personal development

All FM companies conducting either tactical or strategic contracts will need to be on top of developing their staff both in the office and in the field, otherwise they cannot deliver excellence for their clients. FM companies should be receiving very positive feedback from their IiP Assessors (see the Introduction).

Systems for personal development will be created and implemented in all areas of work so that all staff understand the importance of working to the highest standards and are trained to achieve these. Those systems include everything from sales techniques to building a display, from presentation techniques to team management and technical training as necessary – and all this on top of the job procedures and the product knowledge. In the office there will be development too, so that skill sets are improved for the better implementation of activities and so that the staff can see their career path in the industry.

Appraisals

Appraisals will assist in identifying any gaps in an individual's skill set. Steps can then be taken to complete the relevant training.

Managers will also receive training in all areas of employment law and grievance and disciplinary systems, so that they are prepared to treat people correctly and with respect, and know how to discipline any underperformers. This expertise is used both for the field-based staff and for those in the office. (See Chapter 17)

Clients will benefit from this training; they will achieve good results, and have the best motivated staff working on their account. Staff who appreciate that they have a career and are learning can see their routes through to promotion and recognition, and also recognize the client as their partner to achieve this recognition through delivery of goals and targets.

Personnel systems

Staff records

Every FM company will have a personnel system. This system will keep a record of all their field personnel, with information about them, such as their skills and abilities, past experience, training records, uniform size and, obviously, address and telephone numbers. The system is updated as each person works on different campaigns, and thus staff are available to be offered work when any new campaign is implemented.

Employment

Generally, the system in FM is that for each campaign the staff are telephoned or e-mailed, and work is offered to them. The staff have the option of turning down the work, but if they accept it they are expected to adhere to the agreement and get the work completed to a high standard. As in all walks of life, there can be issues and it is the staff who are known to be reliable who will be offered work first.

It is worth reiterating that if an FM agency does not pay well, then the turnover of staff is likely to be higher, Once FM staff are approached by another FM agency (and many of the field staff will work for two or three agencies) then they could dump the lower paid task for the better pay. Clients should be aware of this if they are asking their FM agency to reduce their prices, as up to 90 per cent of the cost of an exercise will be staff-related costs and reductions requested might have to be passed to the staff. (See Chapter 16, where costs of staff churn are discussed.)

Recruitment

The recruitment of staff is an ongoing process in any FM company, whether it is for staff in the office or staff in the field. In the office, the process is as you would expect in any office environment. The specific issues that relate to FM are that there has been a limited resource of experienced FM managers in the industry, as few know the industry exists because it is not on the radar in the academic world. This resource is growing constantly as FM companies train their own staff in-house, and it is largely through the 'grow your own' route that agencies develop their management.

In the field, the recruitment is done usually by region or city. Staff are interviewed and their experience logged and checked, and the data is held on the personnel system at the office. The field staff are trained, usually in the field, by the regional managers and regional trainers who also accompany the staff at work offering further on the job training. Records are kept on the work they have done, and the results and skills shown in the execution of the work, and this builds up the profile for each person, so that they can be booked to the jobs for which they have the relevant skills, or trained to improve their skill sets as appropriate.

Other methods of recruitment of field staff include:

- The internet. There are several web recruitment areas. Some are specifically for FM, but there are many more general recruitment agencies who can also help.
- *The Grocer* magazine.
- Job centres.
- Recruitment agencies.
- Recruit a friend schemes. Reward a current employee if they bring in a friend who works well.

Management

Internal management system (IMS)

One of the issues of running an FM activity for a client is that everything is very fast moving, with daily changes to the logistics and planning. Every FM company must have contingency for what, for example at FDS is morbidly called the 'under the bus syndrome'. FDS have therefore developed their own IMS system internally that keeps every account up to date; thus if an account manager or an account executive is out of the office, sick or on holiday, anyone in the office can get into the person's system and the job will continue seamlessly.

This also ensures that all the steps in an exercise are completed, and has alarm functions fitted to the time plan, so that no deadline can be missed. These alarms extend (after a proper period of time) to a manager, who can then see why the job has not already been done and redeploy staff if necessary.

It is an important part of any business that there is a fluency in the work, but this is never more important than when people are in the field and need to be kept informed at all times.

Appearance matters

Uniforms and costumes

The supply of uniforms or costumes for an FM activity is important, as the uniform can help endorse the brand visibility, credibility and values. These are not items that can be skimped; if uniforms are to be provided they will cost money, and will need to meet certain criteria, be practical and available in sufficient quantity.

The following points are important to remember:

- If staff will be working outdoors (or in an open area) they will need a coat if it is cold or rains. People cannot be expected to stand outside in a T-shirt or sweatshirt in mid-winter in the pouring rain.
- You need to supply sufficient uniforms; if staff are on the road they need at least one on, one off and one in the wash of most items, and two suits or similar in case they spill something. Make sure that a team on the road has plenty of spare clothing. In one case where the client had no spare shirts available bearing the company logo, the staff could not look

their best through no fault of their own, and through no fault of the FM agency.

- Choose the best colour. Avoid white, if the staff have to unpack boxes, deal with newsprint or similar, they are likely to have grubby uniforms for the rest of the day's work.
- Check the sizes. Everyone is not size 'small', nor size 'large'. UK and American sizes are different. Two UK size 10 women were supplied as requested for a campaign. When they arrived at work they saw the costumes, which were a US size 10, equivalent to a UK (tiny) size 6.

Equipment

Typical equipment items might include any combination of the following, depending on the job in hand:

- Presenters. These are used as a tool by FM salespeople to show customers the detail of the product and the exercise that they are conducting. The presenter will contain pictures, text and diagrams to explain the offer which will be designed to help the salesperson make a presentation and a sale.
- Personal data assistants (PDAs), sometimes called hand-held computers (HHC). These devices have a screen on them that will ask for specific information. The operator (an auditor, merchandiser or salesperson) will enter the relevant data for each call, and this information is then transferred to the FM company for analysis.
- Briefcases – to carry all the equipment professionally.
- Cars. It is part of the package with some campaigns to facilitate reliable motoring and vehicles large enough to hold product stocks and POS material.
- Mobile phones – for communication.
- Laptop computers – for communication, record keeping and reporting purposes.
- Uniforms – to give a corporate identity and professional appearance.
- POS or POP material for placing in the outlets visited.
- Toolkit for placing the POS (see Chapter 5).
- Sampling campaign items, for example cocktail sticks, cups, plates, cutlery, paper napkins, hygienic wipes, aprons, hats, black sacks for rubbish and more perhaps, depending on the product.
- Product samples for trial by the business or the consumer.

- Other items for the products, for example coolers to keep drinks cool so that they are sampled at the optimum temperature.

As each campaign is different, the equipment will vary to some degree; the list above gives examples only, and any professional FM company will advise what is needed and will also be able to supply the equipment.

Maintaining a record of equipment items for the field

Records must be kept for all items sent out to the field. The warehouse may not always deal with these records, for example IT might keep track of laptop computers and PDAs, but, nevertheless, there must be a responsibility within the FM company for maintaining records, and thus the return of the items from the field.

Training in equipment use

Policies should be drawn up for the correct use of all items, and sometimes training must be given, and insurances explained where applicable. For example, laptops might not be covered by insurance when the car is unoccupied. Dealing with these issues will be second nature to an FM Company.

Summary

The importance of trained, motivated, ethical staff to FM is a raison d'être of FM. Face-to-face requires two faces: one is the customer, the other the FM brand ambassador representing the personification of the brand. The 2007 customer seeks a relationship with the brand and FM is the way to achieve that. The need to correctly recruit, select, train, reward and motivate such brand ambassadors is a no-brainer. The management of such staff, seeing that their appearance meets the clients' requirements and providing them with the appropriate equipment for the task are also important. What is also not always apparent is to train them in the use of any such equipment, to account for the equipment and ensure that staff are aware of insurance liabilities relating to the equipment.

Self-study questions

10.1. What are the three levels of training carried out by an FM company?
10.2. What is covered in the management of personnel by an FM company?
10.3. Can you list typical items of equipment used by an FM company?

(Answers can be found in the text.)

11 Ancillaries 2

IT and data management, mapping software, warehousing and telephone marketing

The ancillary operations discussed in this chapter are those needed to support the staff in the field, and also to supply the client with detailed feedback and results that will help the client to drive the sales of his or her brand.

Data collection, data management and mapping software are the IT functions that have been developed by FM companies to really make the most of the information collected in the field and to maximize the budget for the client through intelligent reporting. Warehousing and telemarketing are two more support operations that will also help to achieve the best value from the budget, and are used in support of the field staff.

These ancillaries should not be taken lightly; the difference that high standards of support make cannot be underestimated, particularly in the area of data capture and reporting, where FM companies are setting new standards.

IT and data management

FM companies are required to have sophisticated technologies in order to offer the client every advantage in the field, so that any project is well targeted, the correct data is collected and all visits on a client's behalf are monitored and evaluated to give the best ROI.

There are many reasons for this data collection. A few examples follow:

- To establish from an audit the facts in the field at the start of a campaign to be used as a base from which to monitor improvements.
- To chart the growth and developments that are made as a project rolls out.
- To highlight areas of poor performance so that a reason can be established and corrected, for example wholesaler stock issues, geographical preferences.
- To monitor the brand development by store, area, region, for example in terms of distribution, sales, availability, visibility.
- From all this information to develop a meaningful ROI model for the client to evaluate the client's spend.
- To produce actionable reporting, so that issues that are highlighted are dealt with promptly.

The FM Company must be experts at:

- collecting data as per targets or requirement for the task;
- managing and analysing the data collected;
- producing meaningful reports;
- preparing and maintaining lists;
- maintaining internal systems for uninterrupted communication.

Data collection

For accurate data collection the following might be used:

- mapping software with a demographic overlay;
- data collection tools offering real-time web reports;
- a management system.

Mapping software

FDS is one agency that has a system that allows the feeding in of large call files and then produces journey planning, resulting from interrogating the system on one or more of the following:

- Outlet location – collected by address and postcode.
- Gantry details – the name of the store. Is it a symbol store (Co-op, Lidl, Nisa, etc)?

- Store class. What size is the store, and what is the potential for developing this store? The class might be A, B, C or D, or even high, medium, low or poor.
- Store turnover – the value of sales for that store, or for the client's brand in that store.
- Number of product lines stocked. How many of the client's range of products or sizes of product are stocked in the shop?
- Competitor product lines stocked – for all competitors or targeted competitors to measure the status of the client brand by comparison.
- National Lottery. Shops that have a lottery machine have a larger footfall and are usually considered the busiest and largest shops in the area.
- Probability of buying from a car or van. Will staff purchase from a car or van if one calls on them?
- Drinks chiller. Has the store got a fridge or chiller for drinks?
- Post office. If there is a post office, again the footfall will be higher.
- e-POS (electronic POS). Does the store use an electronic method of stock control that will deal with stock replacement of items sold through the till?
- Footfall influence. What is nearby that might increase the footfall, for example schools, hospitals, housing estate, football ground, etc?

Once these details for all the outlets to be visited (say 10,000 outlets) have been fed into the computer, the software will produce a map showing where the calls are in the country. This map is then used for the personnel department to book the staff, so that they are conveniently located near the call clusters, thus saving on travelling time and mileage.

There is an option to select stores by demographic profile, which means that only the stores meeting certain criteria will be selected, such as stores with certain consumer profiles in the vicinity (A, B, C1, etc), or by footprint of a certain store or wholesaler.

Once the staff are all booked to the job, the details are fed into the software again, this time with the staff addresses. Other parameters are fed in too, like the duration of a call, then the software will produce journey plans for each day of work, so that all members of the field team know where they are going each day, how many calls and the order and route to take to fulfil the task. Meanwhile, the office staff know the mileage involved and can thus control costs.

This is the tool that helps with the contact strategy planning critical to achieving good results. The data can be 'sorted' into the categories of outlet, for example prime, standard, secondary and low (A, B, C and D). This division of the calls may decide the frequency of visit and the goals to be achieved in each store type.

This is a most comprehensive planning tool, saving considerable time, effort and costs. It is an expensive tool, yet when well used it saves considerable time and increases accuracy and cost control.

Data collection tools and real-time web reports

Data can be collected by paper on survey forms, via a telephone system or using computer technologies through web reports. In the old days data was entered onto a paper survey form by a field operative and was then captured either manually or scanned. Indeed, there is still manual data capture but only on a very small sample, however, it is much less common for companies to use scanned capture, as, although it is less expensive, it can be very inaccurate.

Collecting data in the field using a paper call survey form and then sending the data from that survey form via a telephone is still used. Interactive voice recording (IVR) is when the completed survey forms for the day are fed into the database via the telephone. Each question on the survey has answers that are given a numeric value, and it is the numeric value that is punched into the telephone keypad in answer to each question.

This can present some problems.

- It can be time-consuming for the field staff when they get home in the evening.
- It is limited in that there is not a text option for commenting.
- With the system being numeric, the answers for the input have to be numeric (for example yes = 1, no = 2).
- Because of the numeric input there is a greater chance of human error if the incorrect number is matched to the answer (with the PDAs the question is 'written' on the screen with a selection of 'written' answers which is much easier and less susceptible to human error).

IVR is best used where brief numeric answers to the survey are required. Nevertheless, this can be a less expensive way of collecting data than using, for example, a PDA. The data from the IVR system can be transferred to the web report.

Currently the most common data capture is by field staff using PDAs (sometimes called hand-held computers: HHCs) or a laptop. With the PDA the questions for the survey are visible on the screen along with a selection of answers, and there is also the option of free text. This makes the PDA the most comprehensive data capture tool, as survey forms are more accurate and give more information via free text.

Complex survey forms can be put on the PDA, and once completed quite simply by the field operator, are despatched via the web to a reporting technology. This includes photographs for each site, so that there is visual evidence of a call.

Matador have also produced an extremely simple system called SWIFT. This is a simplified version of the PDA system, which is used where there is less data to be captured. The advantages of SWIFT are:

- It is very quickly and easily set up.
- It is very easy to use.
- It offers very high accuracy because it is so simple.
- It can be downloaded very quickly after each call.

There are several data capture technologies used. An example is the Matador system used at FDS.

The Matador systems allows real-time reporting. This means that once the data has been collected in the field it is transported to a website where the data is available for those authorized to see it. Matador is so flexible that an account manager can change questions to meet new challenges from the field very simply. An IT input for these variations is not needed, thus saving time and costs. This makes the system particularly flexible to meet the needs of the exercise and the client, as changes can be implemented even as the campaign is running.

All the details collected in the field are downloaded and available virtually immediately on the web, hence the real-time reporting, and different levels of authorized access allow the clients to look at the results at these different levels, either globally or at a regional or an area level.

The demand for data capture

Most demand for data capture is still in the classic areas of availability, distribution, visibility or space and compliance. Client brands want to know if they are getting what has been agreed and how they compare in the areas above against their competitors and against yesterday. This is expected to continue to be the case for the coming years – clients want to get smarter at responding to and improving these core measures before they spend on new forms of data. They therefore want the same data, but delivered in better and new ways.

Increasing areas of demand from client brands are:

- instant visibility of reports;
- deeper analysis to support their decision making processes;
- consistency of data from their agents and their internal field teams;
- multimedia;
- instant alerts of problems;
- feed through of specific data directly to retailers and other channel partners;
- linking of results back to planning systems;
- competitor comparisons.

FM agencies demand:

- greater tracking and visibility of their field teams' activities and plans;
- quick-fire capture for tactical teams;
- multimedia, primarily photographic.

What are changing are the demands of clients' brands on the speed, format and visibility of the data they capture so they can achieve their target of improving the market standard, and this is clearly real-time data with tailored reports and information tables being populated directly from field worker data input.

Managers within client brands want summary views available immediately, formatted in such a way that they can drill down and make rapid decisions. They want action alerts if a measure falls outside of a set standard; they want these alerts instantly, directly from the field and directly to the person who can take action. They want a direct line to data capture in the field rather than data pre-handled by agents.

This form of reporting is very dynamic and it is used to drive the instant daily decisions to achieve the best results with no delays. Clients are finding this tool a very important part of driving the delivery for their brand.

How the data is being used

Data is being used to:

- improve field productivity;
- improve effectiveness and ROI on paid for activities such as promotions;
- drive up compliance of planograms;
- target distribution opportunities;

- compare brand POP factors against competitors;
- negotiate with retailers;
- manage retailer incentive programmes;
- inform the next cycle activity.

Initial advances are being made in FM agencies to:

- measure the net impact of each store visit (both financial and non-financial;
- inform field planning;
- set benchmark models for field team ROI;
- improve the overall returns clients receive from their FM services.

Matador's operational intelligence programme is adding to these uses by bringing retailers and other partners directly into reporting channels, feeding results data straight into planning and operational tools. This allows a more rapid response and finally provides sensitive tracking and data integrity tools to enhance agent and client confidence.

Future developments

Matador's 'operational intelligence' service – a step up from standard 'capture and reporting' – means its clients are already offering their brand clients more in terms of productivity, analysis and market intelligence. They have moved beyond reports into the areas of 'calls to action', better analysis by the merging of results data with other information sources and automated management presentations.

If FM can provide better operational intelligence than clients' brand teams then new market demand for FM agencies will grow. Matador believes this will happen.

The information collected from the field provides a valuable source for assessing the best route forward for any brand, both in the short and long term. Strategies can be realized knowing that regular information harnessed with flexibility in the operations will maximize sales and deliver robust growth.

While the information can be used to track all the elements that might contribute to top class compliance in store, and thus achieve best results (as described in Chapter 6), it is the speed with which the information is transmitted and presented in a digestible form that makes the difference. Gone are the days when the client had to wait a week for the paper to be sorted and reported.

Case study: Matador

Objective

To fully understand the distribution and availability in the independent sector for the client's five brands, one of which has four variants.

The brief

To gain information for **each** store to show:

- current stockists by brand and variant;
- space allocated to each brand and variant;
- competitor products stocked by brand and variant;
- space allocated to each competitor brand and variant;
- size of store and location (near a school, college, football ground, etc);
- space in the store for secondary product displays (dump bins, FSDUs, etc);
- space in the store for POS material, and suggested sizes and type.

Methodology

A full survey form was drawn up that covered all the points above, and the Matador PDAs were loaded up with this information.

Meanwhile the database of stores was cleaned and the 18,000 stores allocated to the exercise put through the mapping software to highlight the call clusters, and field staff were employed to the clusters. The information went back into the mapping software for journey plans for each member of the field team.

The field staff were trained at an attended briefing and the calls were completed. After each call the survey results were sent via the web to the Matador data capture system, where the Matador system automatically generates bespoke reports for the client.

Results

From the data captured it was possible to establish:

- where distribution could be improved;
- where there were opportunities for POS to be placed, and what size and type;
- where dump bins and FSDUs could be placed;
- that the POS was ordered according to the requirements by store;
- the potential of each store so that a target could be set;
- from the targets, an estimated ROI, which endorsed the validity of conducting the roll-out campaign;
- which areas were weak on stocking, and investigations were conducted as to why (for example, wholesaler issues);
- trending over a period of time.

From this campaign a full roll-out for selling the product to the independents and merchandizing the stores was implemented. The surveys on roll-out were also captured via Matador PDAs and the improvements measured against the original data, thus providing the motivation for the field teams and also proving the ROI.

Matador is used for monitoring the ROI models that have been developed for clients, so that this all-important element is regularly reviewed. (See Chapter 14).

Data hygiene

Data hygiene and integrity are an increasingly important focus for FM agencies and their clients. Modern reporting systems include inbuilt field management logs which track the efficacy of the data input, looking especially at the time, logic and location of the field worker at input. The marketing of improved data hygiene and integrity to clients is becoming an increasingly frequent competitive advantage for FM agencies.

Data protection

The laws on data protection are very clear and quite stringent. All UK companies are subject to the restrictions and terms detailed under the Data Protection Act 1998 and must fully understand their obligations under this law. Details can be found on www.ico.gov.uk where the Information Commissioners Office is able to give copies of the Data Protection Act and top tips on how it should be implemented.

For an FM company the main points from this act are:

- When recruiting, all sensitive information must be handled correctly for each job application (age, date of birth, address, etc) and every application should be destroyed after six months.
- All databases must be checked against the preference services (for example the Telephone Preference Service (TPS) so that the people who have registered do not receive unsolicited telephone calls). For all the preference services see the DMA website at www.dma.org.uk.
- All databases must be cleansed every 6 months.

Members of the FMC have to be part of the annual DMA audit on Compliance for the DMA; failure to complete this audit means expulsion from the DMA membership. Therefore, any client using an FMC member knows they are compliant, which is important.

Warehouse and despatch

Distribution

Logistics are a very large part of most FM campaigns, and the logistical support provided in handling the ancillary items is significant in ensuring the success of projects. Ancillary items might include uniforms, POP materials, samples, giveaways, sales presenters, advertising items and relevant equipment (see also Chapter 10).

Most FM companies offer a warehouse and despatch service, so that they can pack and despatch items themselves for distribution to field personnel, retailers and customers as required. An FM company will be much happier to handle their own distribution and to send this to their staff, and then they feel in control of their own destiny. They know how crucial it is to send the correct volume of POS and the correct size uniform, and how time-consuming and costly it is to correct errors. They also understand how mistakes dent the FM company's credibility (and by default the client's).

Similarly, it is better for the FM company to send POS to the staff to take into the store; FM companies' hearts sink when the client insists on sending POS direct to the store. To give a feel for this, generally speaking when POS is sent to the stores as little as 32 per cent of it will be there, and the rest will have been 'lost'; either it has been shoved in a corner and forgotten or damaged, or it has been shredded (see the chart in Chapter 5).

Telephone marketing

Although having lower acceptance and conversion rates than FM, telephone marketing can be less expensive than using people. Field marketers will use the telephone to maximize the FM budget on an 'as and when' basis, making both inbound and outbound calls.

Example 1

The telephone will be used to make sales appointments to specific outlets for a product demonstration or a sales call. This means that the salesperson does not waste time (and budget) going to those businesses for whom the product is not suitable. This telesales might well be conducted by the FM agency, although some agencies may outsource this element. For example, for the selling of utilities to businesses: telesales staff work supporting their own salesperson, making appointments for him or her within the salesperson's territory. The salesperson then goes to the appointment and attempts the sale.

Example 2

In a cycle of visits to outlets, the very large outlets might get a visit from their field ambassador monthly, whereas a smaller outlet would receive a visit quarterly with two telephone calls in the intervening two months, which the field ambassador will also make so that he or she retains the relationship. This stretches the budget, making the contact as economic as possible, as the telephone calls will be less expensive, but it maintains the contact that the field ambassador has with the outlet and keeps the positive CRM.

Example 3

When face-to-face visits are being conducted to independent stores, then the store in the very remote area has its 'visit' conducted on the telephone, as it would be expensive for a person to travel there, and the potential value from the call might not meet the cost of a face-to-face call. Someone trained to the task would make this call, and this might be a regional field manager or an account manager from the office.

A few FM companies are affiliated to or own large telephone marketing companies, so that if there is a large campaign that requires the significant use of the telephone, the telesales part of the exercise will be outsourced to these companies. This is convenient for the client, as the FM company will be able to manage the relationship if required to do so.

Summary

The ancillary activities that are not related to staff concern the entering, recording and transmission of data from any FM activity (particularly auditing and merchandising), the distribution and warehousing of POS materials and other items used for FM (uniforms, equipment, samples) and the use of the telephone (described as telemarketing in the FM industry) to set up visits or to replace visits. This 'telemarketing' itself may be outsourced by the FM agency. All the ancillaries described are areas of growing importance to the FM sector. IT capability now allows the near real-time transmission of data.

Self-study questions

11.1. List 8 of the 12 points that mapping software can offer.
11.2. What might the client reasonably demand from data capture?
11.3. What are the main points for FM on data protection?

(Answers can be found in the text.)

Part 2

Practice

12 How and when to use FM

Part 1 of this book gave an overview of what FM can do in the context of marketing as a whole, starting with a look at the customer then examining the principles and capabilities of each of the FM disciplines and the supporting ancillary disciplines. From here on the emphasis changes to the practical.

Assuming you have acquired a knowledge of FM from Part 1, this chapter and the next four take you through the process of considering how you might best use the FM disciplines through outsourcing some or all of your sales activity to an FM Agency. The thinking before you start the implementation process is covered in this chapter. But it is also important to have an understanding of how an FM agency operates (described in Chapter 13) and to be clear what you want from your investment in FM to achieve, in terms of ROI (in Chapter 14). This leads on to the selection of an FM agency which requires writing a brief and sourcing the agency (in Chapter 15). Working with the FM agency to your best advantage – really also how to get the best out of them, based on lots of experience – is covered in Chapter 16. You should also check on the legal side (in Chapter 17).

Outsourcing the sales function in total clearly gives the best return but it does mean you need to be totally happy with the FM agency you select. There is of course a high level of commercial sensitivity in such outsourcing. Confidence in the ability of the FM agency to retain client confidentiality, to operate with ethical standards and be as good as if not better at sales performance than in-house staff is of paramount importance. The difficulty in finding permission for case studies for this book reflects that sensitivity.

Commercial reality is suggesting that forming partnerships, with 100 per cent cooperation between two parties, does work. As long as there is a trust and openness in the relationship, there should be no difficulty and the doom harbingers that worry about not 'putting all the eggs in one basket' and going with just one supplier may be confounded. The next few chapters are about making the right choice of FM agency.

Chapter 3 indicated what is available to help you from the FM toolkit, whether you come from marketing objectives or whether from a business perspective or a user. In this chapter the options are narrowed down to end up with a precise package of what you are selecting from the FM disciplines to match your particular needs.

Striking a chord

In a book written for a range of readers from different organizations and businesses it is impossible to describe your needs precisely. Through the use of questions with their answers, this chapter is going to try to empathize with you – to strike a chord – to help you identify the parts of the FM disciplines you should home in on to produce a solution suited to your situation.

Remember the advantage of outsourcing the full sales function

The advantage of outsourcing the sales function is that the FM agency is under contract to deliver. This produces a motivation that is hard to reproduce in-house. The sales side of your business then only requires contract management and direction. You are released from the day-to-day commitment of running salespeople, training them, recruiting and employing them, applying best practice, sales planning (other than setting sales targets) and meanwhile you benefit from all the advantages of achieving sales targets and growth without the worry. You can concentrate on the future – new product development, researching how the customer and market is changing and formulating a way ahead. An interim solution is just to cherry pick the parts most suited to FM and then when you see the advantages for real, you move to outsource the whole sales function. It is estimated that up to 15 per cent cost savings can be made through outsourcing the sales function to an FM agency.

Bearing that in mind, consider a range of frequently asked questions to see if any or some might be relevant to you and which FM disciplines might solve them. So, what questions are facing you now?

What needs solving?

See if any of the questions 'strike a chord' and see what FM answers result.

Questions that relate to ROI and budgetary pressure

- Do you want to be able to quantify the investment you are making in marketing your brand?
- Do you want to add significant value to your bottom line?
- Because you are under budgetary pressure, do you wish to justify and defend your marketing spend?
- Do you want to demonstrate in ROI terms just how effective the FM marketing activities that are included in your marketing plan are?

Probably these questions arise because the business is under financial pressure and marketing is the first area where cuts fall. FM disciplines provide a way to be best able to justify your spend to the CEO or financial director in terms of just how much revenue expenditure will produce what return. Here is a prime reason to use the FM disciplines – because of their inherent accountability. Knowing precisely the return against the expenditure that generates this revenue can be a sure-fire winner if results are as predicted or better. Besides, a contract locks in your company and the parts undertaken by the FM agency are protected from attack. There is a whole chapter devoted to ROI (Chapter 14).

The answer

If the pressure is really great, it may make sense to outsource the whole sales function. If that seems too drastic or dramatic then consider just parts of the sales function to outsource, by reading the answers to the questions below. For those parts you do not outsource, look at each marketing activity and set a measurable KPI. That will give you the results providing you ring-fence the activities and give sole responsibility to one person. Mullin (2001) *Value for Money Marketing* gives the detail.

Questions that relate to a product launch

- Are you launching a new product?
- Or a new product variant?
- Or do you want to stimulate sales of a fairly new product for a period?

A new product launch needs to have impact, and as rapidly as possible, to obtain an early return on the development costs. However good the rest of the campaign, without product on the shelves to buy, you will not make sales. As part of your campaign you need intense activity at the POS during the launch period. You need to ensure that shelves are stocked as agreed and the facings correct and POS material in the right place. You need to ensure that the logistics are operating as agreed and the distribution has happened, perhaps also noting the effect on competitors.

The answer

Retail (B2B or B2C)

- Use the FM sales discipline for the launch period.
- Use the FM merchandising discipline for the launch period.
- Use the FM auditing discipline for the launch period.

Service (B2B or B2C)

If you are launching a new service or a service variant or seeking to stimulate the use of a service, in addition to the above, you may need to add mystery shopping to confirm that the service offer is working correctly.

Non-retail (B2P)

If you are a non-retail business or organization for a new course or service then at any event, (member, non- member or a mix of the two) or when responding to telephone callers, use the FM sales discipline to put the offer across and to train in-house staff about the offer and the brand values. Use mystery shopping to confirm that the response is correct. Apply remedial training if not.

Questions that relate to the need to increase volume

- Do you need more sales?
- Does your brand need wider distribution and better visibility?
- Are you looking for a quick fix?

Purely and simply; sales need a boost. You need to encourage more customers to try the product. For non -retail (B2P), this may be a service or a course or training to meet some statutory measure.

The answer

Retail (B2B or B2C)

- Use the FM sales discipline in short bursts at a number of outlets or consider full-time strategic ongoing sales.
- Use the FM merchandising discipline to check that the product is there.
- Use the FM sampling and demonstrating discipline.
- Use the FM experiential marketing, roadshows and events discipline.

Service (B2B or B2C)

- Use the FM sales discipline.
- Use the FM demonstrating discipline.

Non-retail (B2P)

- Use the FM sales discipline.
- Use the FM sampling and demonstrating discipline (depending on the product).

The use of these disciplines will:

- sell in the product or service to the consumer, end-user or member;
- stimulate the trial and sampling of the product to involve and educate the consumer, end-user or member;
- develop brand awareness with the consumer, end-user or member;
- gain distribution through van sales and merchandising in store;
- support the outlets selling the brand to sell it well, with training and incentives to improve sales further;
- respond to market changes by 'tweaking' the activities to meet the changes, even as the activity is running.

Questions that stem from a lack of knowledge of where your brand is

- Do you know what the brand's distribution is?
- Do the competitors have better distribution and visibility?
- Do you know if they do?
- Are your brands distributed across the entire marketplace – through multiples, independents and specialists?
- For some reason the product is not selling too well. It may be certain areas or sectors or types of outlet where you are sure the product has been underperforming. You need facts before you apply a solution.

Is there something about the competitor product or placing that is affecting your sales?

The answer

Retail (B2B or B2C)

- Use the FM auditing discipline.
- Use the FM mystery shopping discipline.

Service (B2B or B2C)

- Use the FM mystery shopping discipline.
- Use the FM auditing discipline.

Non-retail (B2P)

- Use the FM mystery shopping discipline.
- Use the FM auditing discipline.

The use of the disciplines above will:

- establish the facts on product distribution and perception in the market-place;
- establish the facts on competitor activity for analysis on how to counter-act this;
- gain an insight into the weaknesses and strengths of your position and improve the former and develop the latter.

When you have the answer you may then need another FM discipline.

Questions relating to poor performance

- Are you sure your product is presented correctly at the POS so that it is attractive and desirable to the purchaser, is at the correct price, with the correct POS accompaniment, and in the proper section of the store or office?
- Do the people selling your brand in the retail outlets understand it and know the benefits?
- Are you sure the products are a part of a regular ordering and stocking procedure so the brand is never out of stock?
- Are you happy the POS situation is monitored on a daily, weekly or monthly basis in the field using real-time reporting, so that irregular-ities are spotted and sales opportunities maximized?

You may feel that you have a really good product, which the poor perform-ance belies, but you need proof of what is happening on the ground.

The answer

Retail (B2B or B2C)
- Use the FM merchandising discipline with correctional training.

Service (B2B or B2C)
- Use the FM mystery shopping discipline followed later by correctional training.

Non-retail (B2P)
- Use the FM mystery shopping discipline followed by correctional training.

The use of these disciplines will:

- establish the facts on the products' positioning and those of your com-petitor;
- train the staff in store to the products' features and benefits;
- check the ordering and stock processes so that the product is never out of stock;
- maintain high distribution, visibility and sales for the brand;
- for B2P, find out why there is little take-up of what on the surface is a cracking good offer.

Questions to ask if you are unsure of where your brand stands with the customer

- Does the consumer know your brand and value it?
- Do you know the end user's view of your brand?

The answer
Retail (B2B or B2C)
- Use the FM sampling and demonstrating discipline.
- Use the FM experiential marketing, roadshows and events discipline.

Service (B2B or B2C)

- Use the FM sampling and demonstrating discipline.
- Use the FM experiential marketing, roadshow and events discipline.

Non-retail (B2P)

- Use the FM experiential marketing, roadshows and events discipline (at an exhibition, business conference or similar – for whatever target audience you wish to reach).

Using these disciplines will:

- develop brand awareness with the consumer or end-user;
- generate the understanding of brand values;
- involve and engage the consumer or end user so that he or she identifies with the brand;
- allow the product or service to be sampled or trialled to involve and educate the consumer or end user.

If any of the above strikes a chord, then you need FM.

Further thinking

Type of activity – short or long term

Will a one-off blitz suffice, or will you need an ongoing campaign so that you maintain and retain the increases you will achieve? The answer will depend on the size and the urgency of the problem, but generally speaking, a trial in a specific area is the best step, usually for a shorter period (this will depend on the task or the product, but say three to six months). The area could be defined by geography (for example TV area, county, one of your set regions), or by type of outlet to be visited (for example multiples, independent, wholesalers). The area needs to be separately measurable as far as possible. For example, if the trial is being done in the South West, then the sales and distribution for the South West need to be analysed in terms of past sales, current trends etc, so that, when the trial is running and after it has ended, you can measure the difference and thus the effect of the trial.

It would be tempting to conduct a trial in a quiet area, but this might be an area of fewer opportunities. Select an area in which there are opportunities to develop and you will obtain a far better feel for the real value of the exercise.

Once you have established what the trial has achieved, then you can decide whether to extend it, or conduct a series of similar length exercises over wider or different areas.

One point is certain, the management for the client or brand must understand and believe in the exercise, give their unswerving support, and work hard to enhance the results and the sales. Internal fears and jealousies will damage any exercise through lack of information, tools for the job, support and internal negativity.

Once you have proven the working model with a trial, the roll-out can begin. The agency will have the learning from the trial to be able to vary the campaign if this is needed to drive better and higher results. At this point you have a true partner, and provided through monitoring the campaign that the ROI model is populated accurately, you have a very real ability to drive sales forward and money to the bottom line.

Other references

Parts of the some chapters will help with a further understanding of how and when to use FM. Below are a few examples that will help to complete the picture:

- Chapter 16 gives some ideas on making the most of the budget once your procurement of an FM agency has been successful.
- What ancillaries will you probably need? See Chapters 10 and 11.
- What bottom line objectives ROI are trying to achieve? See Chapter 14.
- How will an operation work? See Chapter 13. This chapter will not tell you how to run an FM campaign, but it will help you to understand **some** of the thought processes that have to be gone through to get it planned and then operational. If you read this you will understand more completely the hoops that your FM agency – your FM partner – will need to jump through to make your campaign work, and this will in turn give you a better insight into what you can contribute – it's a two-way street.
- How will you select an FM partner and write a brief? See Chapter 15. This chapter is worth covering as it will help with the approach to an FM company and how you, the client, can gain the best knowledge of the companies more quickly.
- Chapter 4. Parts of this chapter will also assist in the how and when to use FM, as it deals with the maintenance of advantage, retention of the long-term gains in a strategic contract and the erosion of advantage in the independent retail sector after short-term bursts.

Summary

This chapter has tried to help to develop the thinking of what specifically you might outsource to an FM agency. FM can help with confirming, or otherwise, a feeling perhaps you have about poor sales figures and what might be done to resolve that. FM can clearly assist with high points in a brand's life such as with a product launch, but it may also help a relaunch or a launch to a new target audience. How well trained and motivated are your in-house staff? You might wish to try some FM sales support to see how effective highly trained staff are. You may wish to test the suggestion that the 2007 customer seeks to experience the brand, and arrange a roadshow or series of events to allow brand experience. The purpose of the chapter is to set you thinking so that you have an idea of what you might outsource in the short or long term.

Self-study questions

12.1. Make a list of marketing problems that occur in your organization.

12.2. Against the list put the FM disciplines that might solve the problems.

12.3. What 'further thinking' areas does this chapter suggest?

(Answers can be found in the text.)

13 FM in operation

Understanding the FM agency

'Chicken and egg' – how an FM agency operates – helps to write the brief

The FM agency has to be briefed on what a client wants from them and in quite some detail, to be able to put a project in place and implement it. In order to write a brief that will really make life easy for both parties – client and FM agency – it is necessary to have a pretty good idea of the culture and understand how an agency operates. This chapter does just that – from the moment that the FM agency has been awarded the project.

The FM agency first produces a plan that is agreed with the client. The project has to be managed particularly, finding training and employing staff, both from the office and operationally in the field. Venues have to be selected. Then the project starts.

In the beginning

The preliminaries to starting a project

The process of how an agency is selected is described in Chapter 15. In essence, after the telephone call and the receipt of a brief, the FM agency produces a proposal with costings. This is compared with other competitor submissions and a shortlist is drawn up. Then approximately two or three FM agencies are interviewed. There may be further activity but, from all this, an FM agency is selected. That is the point where this chapter begins. The FM agency has won the project and after a short period of euphoria the hard work begins.

Clarifying the brief

From the brief (covered in Chapter 15) and then probably a further two or three days of meetings with the client after the project has been awarded, the brief is fleshed out into a lot of detail, from which the agency develops a project plan. Once the project plan is agreed with the client that becomes the 'bible' and it is this document that is then implemented by the FM agency and the client.

By this stage there should be a contract between the client and the FM partner, clarifying the work to be done, the responsibilities and legal commitments. There are times when the contract will take some time to be prepared, and it is not unusual for work to start before this is finally agreed and signed.

Starting with the plan

The project plan

The planning is probably the most important part of any project. The project plan should be very detailed for each and every step and show:

- who is responsible for each single step (client, FM agency, third party);
- the time frames for each step to be completed;
- the exact delivery date for each step.

The plan should be written carefully, and copied to the client and closely discussed with the client, so that everyone is comfortable and that all the items are covered. A key point is that all must be happy with their responsibilities and know what and when they must deliver. The FM company should ensure that the objectives and processes are realistic and advise on the critical time path.

Any user of FM should be aware that not sticking to the plan could have an adverse knock-on effect for the project, and either spoil, delay or cause extra costs. A field marketer should never allow a plan to run behind time, therefore it is important that the plan is realistic.

The project plan will also detail timings and deadlines for all or some of the following:

- the preparation and production of a call file – the list of outlets to be visited, with detail such as:
  - what the file needs to contain: outlet name, address, telephone and fax numbers, e-mail, map, access; also outlet classification, size, shape, layout;
- where it is coming from (the client, etc);
- who will provide it (which department or division, etc);
- what format it needs to be in (software program);
- how it will be graded for use (security access, levels of access);
- geographical overlay or profiling (all outlets, by product ranges, by size);
- demographic overlay if required by area;
- call routing and journey planning for field staff;
- when the file will be available if the client is supplying it (the FM company may already have a suitable database);
- staff allocation, recruitment:
  - staff from FM agency database, selected and employed to the project;
  - detailed full recruitment programme, where applicable (also to cover staff shortfalls), including date of advertisements through to interview venue and date, etc;
- training:
  - head office account team;
  - field manager job description and training (areas, tasks, responsibilities);
  - field executive job description and training (outlets, tasks, responsibilities, training programme authors, training programmes – content, type of training; schedule – date, place and time of delivery);
  - use of any equipment or tools for training;
  - use of any products, presenters, PDAs, POS for training;
- equipment or tools:
  - presenters, PDAs, briefcases, cars, mobile phones, uniforms, POS, toolkit, plates, cups, etc (see Chapter 10 for descriptions);
  - details of who will supply these and exactly when;

- venues or place of work:
  - locations selected and booked, if appropriate;
  - special rules for each location detailed;
  - deliveries to the venues;
- working practices or controls:
  - for the field, taken from job descriptions, contracts, operations manual, incentives, call procedure, reviews, appraisals, targets, etc;
  - for the client's ROI model, strategic reviews;
  - for the FM agency KPIs, service level agreements (SLAs), reconciliations, technology, etc;
- reporting or results (the key deliverables);
  - tools and methods of reporting (including establishing base points);
  - design of the report to meet the client's requirements and track KPIs and SLAs to measure ROI and decide the key deliverables to be input to the ROI model (see more on this in Chapter 14);
  - reports for the FM company to analyse, recommend, management reports, etc, against a timetable of, say, weekly and monthly intervals, project milestones;
  - dates for the review meetings.

Time should be allowed for the plan to be drawn up, so that it is thorough.

When short-notice campaigns become difficult to control and monitor, it is usually because there was insufficient time for comprehensive planning.

This master plan is presented either as a date or time ordered list or as a Gantt chart. It should be one of the standards set in the SLAs that the timings on the chart are honoured as a matter of course by all parties.

Even the little things matter, for example a junior member of the client team was given three days to approve a training document for a training session in Manchester. Despite constant reminders the approved copy was received at 5.00 pm on the fourth day. The training course was the next day in Manchester. The account team had already had to leave the office to drive to Manchester at 4.00 pm so that they could set the room and prepare. By the time the substantial training manuals had been copied by other colleagues at the office, passed to a courier and driven to Manchester, it was 2.00 am. The young client hadn't had time to read the document as she was having a farewell lunch with one of her colleagues. Of course the worst part of this was the extra cost of late work and a courier to Manchester, for which there

Client Project Plan

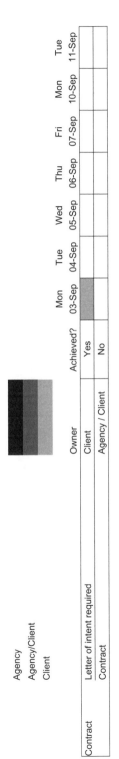

Legend:
- Agency
- Agency/Client
- Client

	Owner	Achieved?	Mon 03-Sep	Tue 04-Sep	Wed 05-Sep	Thu 06-Sep	Fri 07-Sep	Mon 10-Sep	Tue 11-Sep
Contract									
Letter of intent required	Client	Yes	▨						
Contract	Agency / Client	No							
Meeting dates									
Initial Meeting	Agency / Client	Yes	▨						
Weekly project planning meetings	Agency / Client	No						▨	
Call File									
Call file to be received	Client	Yes		▨					
Ideal territories to be mapped as per call file	Agency	Yes			▨				
Call schedule to be agreed with callage dates	Agency	Yes				▨			
Core team to be identified	Agency	No							
Reporting / Results									
Agree specific reporting requirements with Client	Agency / Client	No						▨	
Discuss and agree KPIs	Agency / Client	No						▨	
Discuss and agree SLAs	Agency / Client	No							
Set up questions on handhelds, 2 day lead time	Agency	No							▨

Figure 13.1 Sample project plan

was no budget. Had the approved document been received on time, then copies would have been produced in working hours and would have travelled in the car with the attending managers.

Contingency

All plans should have a contingency in case something does not happen as expected. All staff at an FM agency are typically trained in contingency planning, and for large projects a contingency budget would exist.

One of the roles of FM people is to seek out all the 'What if ...?' questions, see what contingency they will need to deal with these, and then have the resource and training to cope with unexpected or unconsidered 'What if ...?' issues.

Project management

Management in the office

Every company will have their own hierarchy, but the one following is probably fairly typical. Of course not all campaigns will involve all levels of staff, although the large ones will. The hierarchy will vary from one company to the next, but the following chart probably shows the most usual structure in the office. The senior directors are responsible for driving the strategy, and staff below them will deliver the operational aspects of the campaign.

Office management

Managing director

Client services directors

Client services managers

Senior executives

Junior executives

Figure 13.2 Hierarchy

The office is a very lively, bubbly place to be; nothing is the same two days running and the constant pressure of work keeps everything moving at a fair old pace! The members of the account teams work in a group and their numbers depend on the volume of work involved in the project. Other people involved in any project are:

- Sales division, who seek out the work and present the quote – the proposal with costings – to the client.
- Finance division, who assist with quotes, sort out the payments and invoices, run the payroll, deal with NI and PAYE for many people, plan the cash flow and do the accounts.
- Personnel division, responsible for booking the staff and maintaining the personnel database accurately and highlighting training needs.
- IT division, as detailed previously (in Chapter 11).
- Trainers. Training is conducted for every single exercise, and can take the form of either a postal briefing or an attended briefing. The trainers have to book venues, invite the staff and prepare the training documents and deliver the training. They must also be very aware of the personal development of all staff, both in the field and in the office and make recommendations to the directors and the HR department.
- HR department. With the ever more complicated issues in employment law this department spends time ensuring that contracts for all staff are correct, the Employee Handbook is up to date, and that all staff problems and grievances are dealt with correctly. The HR department also deals with keeping the intranet up to date, and is also involved with people development, maintaining the IiP standards and so on.

Field staff selection

So that a client can expect properly experienced and trained staff, who will correctly represent the brand, all FM companies will have a database of staff. This database typically includes a personnel programme that contains all the details, including, for every individual listed, experience, training received, full personal details, a recent photograph (or recent video) and any special skills such as juggling, face painting, rollerblading, painting and decorating or cookery, so that individuals can be selected for specific tasks where their skills are needed. A health and safety certificate will need to be held by anyone who works with food sampling.

Holding these details means that staff can be selected to meet the profile of the job in hand. For example, biscuit sampling needs someone who looks as though he or she is a person who cooks and eats biscuits and knows what he or she is talking about, whereas nail varnish promotion needs a more sophisticated person with nice nails, shampoo promotions need people with nice hair, and so on; also staff need to be qualified for the job, in terms of experience and training, just as in any other area of employment. This is not dissimilar to TV adverts except a higher standard is required overall, for where a TV advertisement will show the perfect hands of one person then they may use a different person's legs and a different face, the FM brand ambassador has to be all in one.

A specific word of warning about staff selection – the Age Discrimination Act makes it very difficult to recruit staff of a specific profile in terms of age, so it is important that when selecting the staff the FM agency allow staff of all ages to apply for a position.

IT-based staff booking systems have been developed to reject a double booking, and with often over 1,000 staff out each week, an IT-based system is a valuable tool!

There are other ways of recruiting staff which are more usually used for strategic long-term contracts and as well as using their own database an FM agency might also use:

- internet recruitment sites;
- job centres;
- *The Grocer* magazine;
- a recruit a friend scheme – an incentive to current staff to put friends forward;
- advertisements in local newspapers.

Operational project management

Field management structure

Similarly, in the field the structure might not be used at every level. Again this depends on the numbers of brand ambassadors out in the field, and their geographic location. Job titles too may vary.

Some of the field staff will be exclusive to one campaign, and others, such as the regional field managers (RFMs), may well be retained by the FM company to deliver across several campaigns in their region. The

RFMs and their staff supply essential feedback on the task in hand, and methods and approach in the field can be varied. This offers flexibility which helps achieve better results.

Area field managers (AFM) will support the RFMs when required, and team leaders (supervisors) will run teams, where a concentrated team effort is applicable. This is usual on a roadshow, for example, when the team leader will ensure that everything runs smoothly on a daily basis.

A typical field management structure in an FM agency is shown below.

The case study describes a typical example of a day's work for an FM brand ambassador.

Field management

National field manager

Regional field managers

Area field managers

Team leaders

Brand ambassadors

Figure 13.3 Field management structure

Case study: A day in the life of a campaign executive

7.30 am – Quick glance in the mirror. Pick up the laptop, have I got everything with me for the day? Yes! Climb into the car and crawl through traffic to the first appointment of the day.

8.45 am – Arrive at the retail outlet to deliver a training session on the client's products and services. A presentation at a recent area manager meeting highlighted the need for training in this branch.

11.00 am – At the end of the training I spoke to the store manager and with his help set up an incentive between the two new starters I had just trained. Booked to come back next month to measure achievement.

11.15 am – Back in car and off to 'phonetalk' where I have negotiated to remerchandize the whole window to the client's colours. Arrive and unload all the POS from boot and have a quick catch up in store with the manager to make sure all's OK for me to proceed.

12.45 pm – Take a photograph of the display. I can use this for the incentive – might win top prize! Just time for a quick bite with the girls in the staff room and then, much refreshed, hot foot it to next appointment.

1.10 pm – Must get a move on, going to meet the sales manager of a big distributor, appointment booked for 2.00 pm. I am the day-to-day contact for them, acting as a buffer for the account manager, sorting problems and keeping the relationship on track. Agreed action plan for developing three underperforming stockists.

4.00 pm – Back in my car, another three voicemails and two text messages to answer. Some are from store managers with issues but two of them from colleagues wanting to share experiences of the day.

4.30 pm – Drive to my last call of the day, presenting new objectives to staff in a retail outlet.

5.15 pm – Back home to type up reports for the training session and check the distributor meeting notes, all to be e-mailed today to the office.

Drive past the window I created earlier. It's attracting lots of attention.

Job done, I wonder what tomorrow will bring?

RFMs are also 'on the spot' to deal with any difficulties, including personnel issues, as field people have the same problems that we all have from time to time – sickness, cars broken down and children ill. The RFM might also cover for someone in the RFM's area should the need arise.

In the sales environment the team leader and the RFM would be responsible for accompanied sales calls with the sales staff to ensure that they are selling to their potential, and are ultimately responsible for the sales targets being met. In the sales environment, the job titles will change for staff dedicated to the task, for example area sales manager, sales executive.

The number of staff and managers working on any project will vary according to the project in hand and its size. As a client it is wise to understand the field management and their job functions in relation to your requirements in the field and in relation to the logistics and the complexity of their implementation in the field. Activities vary, but bear in mind that skimping on the field management is not usually wise.

Choosing venues

Venues and targeting the audience

This usually applies to tactical work but if a strategic partner is conducting work, the same principles will apply.

Defining the target market for a product or service is pretty fundamental to brand development; so selecting the venue where there are plenty of opportunities to meet those targeted is important, and should not be too difficult.

Many venues require significant notice of an activity, and some are booked as much as a year ahead, so pre-planning is crucial. These venues are often looking for their visitors to be entertained, without giving their visitors any hassle, so attractive activities that have some theatre attached to them are well considered. This is particularly true of shopping centres, railway concourses and theme parks, although others also like to inform or amuse.

All venues have to be paid for, and it is important that the venue carries the level of footfall and the right profile to justify the cost of being there. An FM company will help you with the decisions on this. For example, venues might include universities, motorway service areas, car parks, the outside vicinity of large stores, business parks and industrial estates, places of entertainment for holidaymakers or the seafront.

Everywhere needs permission; even working in the street requires the permission of the local council. The methods of gaining approval from the different types of venue can be different from one venue to the next, and it would be impossible to go into all the detail in this book; however a good FM company will steer you through all the various requirements for the different locations.

The project starts

Implementation

Every project in FM is unique, and so the implementation will vary accordingly. It would be impossible to go through every possible scenario of project implementation, but the main requirements are detailed below, and these will generally not vary. The project-specific detail will be built into the carefully constructed project plan, and the FM company will be responsible for driving this forward. The client will have action points too, and will have to adhere to the delivery within the time frames detailed or the project will be held up.

Sample implementation of a project

For this example assume a strategic force is being put out to deliver sales and merchandising nationally to a very large number of retail outlets.

The FM company responsibilities during the project are:

- implementing the project or campaign according to the objectives and timing agreed;
- auditing the results;
- obtaining the best financial results (meeting the budget);
- devising the relevant report according to the client's requirements;
- advising on added benefits (see Chapter 16);
- extending the value of the operation.

In the office

Account managers will sort out the data by:

- deleting unwanted calls;
- overlaying any demographic requirements;
- putting the calls in areas of work;
- developing journey plans for staff (once they know where the staff live who are doing the job), thus controlling time and mileage in the field.

Personnel will deal with staff issues:

- writing job descriptions;
- selecting the staff by area;
- arranging the training venues;
- writing the training manuals.

IT will deal with data capture and reporting:

- writing the reporting function so that this is robust and captures the required information in the field;
- arranging for the availability of equipment from their department (laptops, PDAs, etc);

- ensuring that the training or operating instructions for the equipment is correct;
- planning the reporting process, so that data from the field is accurately logged and the reports will be according to the client's requirements.

Other equipment will need to be sourced by account managers – cars, presenters, uniforms (see Chapter 10). The finance department will add the project staff to their payroll.

Meanwhile, the strategic directors or client services directors will be:

- ensuring that the strategy is being driven through by the actions being taken and offering advice and help with the operational departments to ensure that the strategy is on target;
- overseeing the collation of reports as required by the project plan to meet project milestones or weekly and monthly reporting times as agreed in the project plan.

The warehouse staff will be collecting all the items required and:

- storing them until the training day;
- sending the necessary items to training;
- storing the balance of items for future work.

In the field

RFMs will be:

- assisting with recruiting in their area;
- conducting some early analysis on sample outlets to be visited;
- attending the training course to meet and motivate their staff.

Once the training day arrives:

- The office and field staff meet at the training.
- The staff are all given their training and their instructions.
- The field staff are given their equipment.

Then:

- Field staff conduct the work.
- Field managers will help them; audit work, do quality checks and generally ensure the smooth running of the project in their area.

- Account managers (and their team) will support the field and monitor the success of the project:
  - dealing with any difficulties;
  - advising on how to overcome problems;
  - doing all the necessary administration for the smooth running of the project;
  - checking the reports and passing these to an analyst for interpretation;
  - checking staff expenses and pay;
  - dealing with personnel issues, or passing these to HR;
  - maintaining daily contact with the client;
  - seeking ways to improve or perfect the project;
  - carrying out field visits to see things for themselves.
- Strategic directors will maintain an eye on the entire project to see what value can be added, and to check that the project is in line to deliver the required strategy.

Account managers will also be the guardians of the purse strings, and ensure that budgets are not exceeded.

Case study: A day in the life of an account executive

7.00 am – Leave home to meet a new installer. My main task for the day is to train a new member of field staff so that she can effectively represent both client and agency out in the field.

8.00 am – Traffic is hell as usual so I've left plenty of time to get there. I arrive with 15 minutes to spare so I have a last check over my briefing notes and refresh on the key training points.

9.00 am – New installer on board and we are now underway.

9.45 am – Time to locate the home of the previous installer to pick up the POS. Glad I have a co–pilot with an A–Z!

10.05 am – Sit down in the back of the car, POS onboard.

10.10 am – First store, East Finchley here we come!.

10.35 am – Parked up, now travelling to the store on foot armed with the POS. Need to purchase some disposable cameras en route so that we can photograph the installation for the client. We try to buy cameras in three shops but they only take cash, and there are no banks in sight!

11.00 am – Arrive at the store and greet the store manager. Take the installer through the store planogram and explain what is required in store. Silly hat time – as we are in the food preparation area placing posters in the menu boards above the counter, hygiene hats need to be worn. With the POS installation complete, en route to Kilburn store.

11.25 am – Driving through Camden Town. Pulled over onto a double pavement, here's a store not due to be called upon until tomorrow but as we are passing may as well complete the POS installation now. Keeping eyes peeled for traffic wardens. Offered free food and drink from the store and I'm hungry but there's no time to stop. The new installer is an experienced merchandiser and a fast learner and seems confident with the installations – good news for me as I need strong team members out in the field.

11.35 am – Continue on to Kilburn after the unplanned stop.

11.50 am – Arrive at Kilburn, nowhere to park. I drop off the installer with the POS at the store. I circle Kilburn to park while she installs the POS. Check the installation and all is fine. Lucky she is a fast learner.

12.20 pm – On to Collingdale, last call of the day.

12.40 pm – Parked just round corner from the store – fantastic, a bit of luck at last. Posters up and we were away.

1.00 pm – Training completed, on the way back to drop off the installer. Have a meeting at 3.00 pm back at office. Plenty of time to get back, or so I thought.

2.15 pm – Still trying to get out of London, traffic is a complete nightmare. No chance of attending the meeting now! Phone to apologize for absence.

3.30 pm – Finally back at the installer's car, time to summarize the day's key points and transfer all the POS to installer's car ready for her to go it alone tomorrow.

4.00 pm – En route to the office. My stomach is rumbling. I haven't eaten all day.

4.30 pm – Arrive back at the office 30 minutes before the staff meeting. Just enough time to check e-mail and catch up on the day's events.

5.00 pm – Food! Buffet in the staff meeting – lifesaver.

5.15 pm – Sit down; ears open, listening to what is happening in other areas of the company.

6.00 pm – Quick drink after the meeting, time to go home ready for another eventful day tomorrow.

All of the above is happening at the same time, and many people will work to meet the timing deadlines imposed by the project plan, so that the project starts on time.

All projects are different, and will not mirror the detail set out above; this is a sample only, to give the reader an idea of what might be done to achieve a plan.

SLAs

These agreements are between the client and the agency, and define responsibilities and the standards that will drive the partnership (see Chapter 16).

Summary

Understanding the operation of an FM agency helps with the writing of a briefing document when selecting an agency to carry out FM tasks. The FM agency (once tasked and with contracts in preparation), after detailed questioning of the client, prepares a project plan. This is the working document to which the FM agency operates. The team is recruited and selected to match the project needs with a management hierarchy tailored but able to report to the client on project progress as it meets project milestones or routine timelines as agreed.

Self-study questions

13.1. What are the main elements that make up a project plan?
13.2. How is a project managed, from both the office and field perspectives?
13.3. How is a project implemented in the office and in the field?

(Answers can be found in text.)

14 Measuring FM's success – ROI

FM's truly powerful monetary position

With FM you can see the effect of activities quickly, in currency, as an immediate increase in sales and faster than with other forms of marketing. Assuming you know how much you have spent to achieve this revenue and the return, ROI can be shown. This is not a function that is implemented for an accountancy definition, this is merely a formula that allows the client and the FM agency to establish what a piece of expenditure has delivered in returns in a simple, measurable way. It is a formula that allows clients to include their own internal methods of justifying the spend too, as each ROI model varies from one client to another. Clients and FM agencies alike constantly use the term ROI, which is the marginal increased contribution generated with the costs of the campaign deducted.

Once an ROI model has been drawn up, the work is conducted, and the various elements that contribute are loaded into the ROI model. This will then produce the ROI, which (it is hoped) will match the returns that were estimated.

However, the process does not stop there; the ROI will be ratified by checking data, for example checking Nielsen to see if market share has increased, independent audits of 'sales out ' data and the pull-through from stores, cash and carry outlets or wholesalers. Thus the veracity of the ROI can be checked, and the target outcome can be monitored and adapted if necessary.

Using the ability to measure FM activities against the return, it is possible for the astute, using a number of techniques – accumulated from the vast experience of FM agencies – to predict the estimated outcome of an FM project against its cost (revenue expenditure) and when that predicted outcome or better is achieved, benefit from the accolades that follow. The predicted outcome is defined through the ROI model agreed between the FM agency and the client.

This chapter aims to help clarify some of the points that will help you to predict what you can expect to achieve in ROI when you appoint an FM agency to carry out a project. The next chapter deals with the selection and procurement process. The FM agency is there to make you money – but how much should you expect the agency to make for you, against what outlay? Is this entirely a win-win situation? Examples are given in this chapter as to what you might expect. Remember that this is an area of particular commercial sensitivity too. It should, however, be possible to predict reasonable figures. ROI on different types of campaign will differ as there are variables that will affect it. For example, ROI on a campaign to independent retailers will differ from ROI achievable in the multiple stores.

As FM uses staff extensively there is a high cost (revenue expenditure) but the returns are equally substantial and rewarding. Management may feel the investment is high but that has to be offset by the higher expected returns. In this commercially sensitive area you will need to be guided by the FM agencies you have chosen to pitch for your project. Current clients do not reveal either investment or return and information on this is closely secured within the confidentiality agreement signed by the FM company (most usually) at the start of the pitching process and later in the contract. FM agencies will have a view on what you might receive on ROI, based on previous experience, and estimates can be drawn up. By outsourcing the sales function you can expect a near guaranteed return to the levels agreed jointly in the ROI model drawn up together.

ROI

FM, with all its disciplines, is the winner for measuring ROI. No other part of marketing so clearly provides the returns that can be achieved.

ROI can be measured by the contribution made to the client's profits, by achieving goals that are known to drive sales. These goals might be improved availability, increased distribution, direct sales, numbers of samples distributed, improved brand awareness generated to improve sales and the achievements of KPIs by the sales force, when these KPIs reflect the known drivers that achieve sales and, therefore, profits. Having gathered the data, it is then converted into a contribution that is measured by a monetary value. This is known in the FM jargon as the ROI model.

The case study examples below, achieved with two clients, demonstrate how to establish the profit-building KPIs.

Case study: ROI 1

In independent retailers, gaining an average of two extra distribution points per outlet on the shelves, won for a client by the FM agency through applying the merchandising and (ex-car) sales disciplines to a wide number of stores. This gave a predicated annual profit of £500,000 after just two months' activity.

Calculation

Number of new lines: 2
Average rate of sale of line when in distribution: 0.5 cases a week
Measured contribution per case: £4.50
Number of stores: 2,000
$2 \times 26 \times £4.50 \times 2,000 = £468,000$

Case study: ROI 2

Improving the distribution of a range of products through applying the sales, merchandising and auditing disciplines in only one grocery sector, after all costs were covered, put a seven-figure sum to the bottom line (ie profit) in 10 months.

As previously stated, the model for measuring ROI should be in place before work begins, although it may well change during the campaign as the client and agency develop the work. It should be one of the project objectives alongside the plan. Research conducted by the client and/or the FM agency, both drawing on their experience, will show the areas on which to concentrate, and together they can set KPIs that are realistic and profitable for the client. The client will have to reveal the figures for the rate of sale and the profit for the product will also need to be known, as these are critical parts of establishing ROI.

The ROI model

Once these criteria are established, the ROI model can be drawn up. The FM company will impart the KPIs through training to their FM field force. Constant monitoring and review will show the returns being achieved and the ROI, but will also show the improvements made to any one outlet over a series of visits, which is a great indicator that the field brand ambassador has developed a relationship with the client. These relationships are important, as the retailer now has an understanding and affiliation with the brand, and will continue to purchase the brand for as long as that relationship exists.

An ROI model is just a series of calculations made on figures that have been achieved in the field, and actions taken that are known to drive sales. The KPIs will provide some of the figures to be fed into the model to make the calculation for ROI, thus to build an ROI model you will need to be aware of the sales fundamentals that are the target to be achieved in store, often referred to as compliance. These include:

- agreed stocking of the range (in all its variants);
- agreed number of facings;
- correct price point displayed;
- visible, prominent agreed shelf position;
- SELs in place;
- correct BSEs.

Once these fundamentals are in place, the following can be worked on:

- additional displays (FSDUs, secondary, Gondola end and stack displays);
- extra facings;
- extra POS (carried by the merchandiser just in case they are not available in store).

Predicting an ROI can be brave, as there are variables that might ruin the model as the work progresses. These might include (although not exclusively):

- The competitors fielded a campaign that spoilt the drive and thus the ROI.

- There was a price increase for the product, making it less competitive and attractive.
- For a new product launch, the rate of sale at trial was not achieved on the roll-out, so ROI suffered.
- Targets were set too high to be achieved in the field.

The achievement of the KPIs at a high standard will influence the good effect of the ROI when these figures are calculated into the ROI formula.

Marketing accountability

If you believe that marketing is an investment, you need to be able to prove this. Many companies over the past years, when making cuts, have immediately hit the marketing budgets, (and FM is most usually funded through the marketing budget). If you can prove ROI you can also prove the value of marketing to your board, which is becoming an essential part of the internal company reporting. No other marketing discipline so clearly outlines the returns that can be achieved than FM.

In simple terms, FM ROI is:

The **profit** from	minus	the cost of gaining
extra sales made		those extra sales
		(the revenue
		expenditure budget)

This shows the value of the increased sales, and shows what the brand has achieved for the money it has spent.

Note that when an FM financial proposal is accepted by a client this includes the costs for the **entire exercise**, (field staff, management, office administration, meetings, etc) thus when cost of sales is shown, this will include all the costs.

Very occasionally there are times when the only objective is to gain market share; this is calculated differently.

The **value** of the ÷ the total market × 100 = % market share
extra sales made   gained

The ROI model is built by also including the elements of the task that can be measured by the contribution made to the client's profits by achieving goals that are known to drive these profits. These goals might be:

- increased distribution;
- in-store compliance (see above);
- higher sales;
- samples distributed;
- awareness generated (which can be measured when coupons are given out and subsequently redeemed, or in increased sales as the relationships are developed and the loyalty to the brand increases).

The aim is to improve sales and the achievements of KPIs by the sales force, when these KPIs reflect the known drivers that will achieve profits.

Field personnel in the outlets deliver the objectives and collect the data. Having gathered this data it should be analysed and the results and achievements can convert into a contribution that is measured by a monetary value.

The data to load into the ROI model

The data collected from each store will be loaded into the ROI model, and the effects and improvements monitored. The data that will be used to build the ROI model will include an appropriate selection of the following:

- sales made;
- sales retained over a specific period (customer loyalty);
- sales fundamentals, as detailed above;
- retention of these sales fundamentals over a given period;
- increased facings or secondary displays;
- POS placed;
- calls made per day;
- achievement of KPIs by field staff;
- new stores added to the database (increased distribution);
- compliance with incentive schemes sold to retailers to retain brand presence and loyalty.

For methods of data capture, see Chapter 11.

Given that all the actions detailed above will drive sales, and therefore profits, a value can be given to each action, and the specific ROI model for the client is built. This does involve the client sharing some confidential information with their FM company, as the profits and ROI can only accurately be measured if the margins on a brand are known. Given the close relationship between the client and the FM agency, and given that they both have the same goals to achieve, we have not known this to be a problem.

An FM agency will have experience of ROI models, and will be able to build one that will define what the activity has done for the bottom line for the brand. This is a very valuable, ongoing exercise, as this will highlight how the different areas of the work affect the brand's development, and changes can be implemented to improve the results.

ROI on sampling

Perhaps the most difficult area for ROI is in the sampling arena, and this could apply to experiential marketing and roadshows too. This is because it is difficult to precisely quantify exposure; that does not mean that the work is not worthwhile, after all many companies have huge spends in this more unquantifiable area – TV and bus shell advertising to name but two (although this is changing now) – but a client looking for a precisely measured return should be aware of this.

Of course, adding money-off coupons to samples and checking redemption, and checking purchase in local stores, before, during and after a sampling campaign, will help identify uplifts in sales, and thus ROI can be determined. The involvement, brand awareness and loyalty engendered by the sampling activity will count for a great deal, but precisely how much will not be tangible.

One method of estimating a potential ROI on sampling might be:

- Know the profit margin of the product being sampled, for example £1.
- Estimate how many purchases a year a customer might make of the brand (say five, therefore £5 per converted customer per year).
- Calculate how many customers you need from the exercise to break even given the cost of the campaign, for example: the campaign costs £10,000 ÷ £5 = 2,000 customers.
- Evaluate whether the campaign will give 2,000 customers, if say 20,000 samples are being distributed, will a 10 per cent conversion rate be achieved? Is this likely?

But be aware that this is not the whole story; there is a great deal of awareness that will be engendered by the activity, so more people than have been sampled will be aware of the brand and recognize it, and this will have a positive effect too, even if it cannot be precisely measured.

Examples of ROI

The following are examples which, although real, have been 'sanitized' for this book

Case study: ROI 3 – utilities business

750,000 extra sales achieved from four counties of England in three years (each contract will have an average lifetime value profit).

Average lifetime profit:
Average annual usage of electricity in sterling:
Plus average annual usage of gas in sterling:
Less cost of generation or wholesale cost:
Less administration costs:
Multiplied by the average length of customers loyalty in years
= Contribution or ROI
Result: 750,000 × average lifetime value profit, less costs of sales drive = ROI

Case study: ROI 4 – retail product

A new variant of a product that had cost significant amounts to develop was about to be de-listed by a multiple because sales were so low. An audit found that only 34 per cent of stores were stocking the new variant, and not the 100 per cent stocking that was expected, and against which the product was being judged, hence the low sales.

Result: The product is still listed, and is a 'must stock' for the multiple now. The value of a must stock line can only be guessed at over the past six years throughout a major multiple – it must be very substantial though!

Case study: ROI 5 – retail product

Activity: implementing a strong category management campaign into multiple grocery outlets for one sector only.
Result: sales in that sector uplifted by 20 per cent year on year.

Case study: ROI 6 – service product

Activity: Selling a contract for a large institution.
Result: It was judged by the client that two sales per person per day would pay for the exercise, and any extra sales on this would be profit for the client. A target was set of four sales per day, and the average achieved was 7.8 sales per person per day.

Merchandising versus no merchandising

Significant research was carried out with one client comparing the quality of their in-store merchandising and their sales both when there was FM agency merchandising discipline coverage and when there was no FM agency merchandising discipline coverage.

The chart below is for a major multiple (with different stores and a different brand from the example in Chapter 5). The top part of the chart shows the **out of stocks** that occur when a field ambassador is regularly visiting the stores for one product. The bottom part of the chart shows the out of stocks when the field ambassador was not visiting the stores.

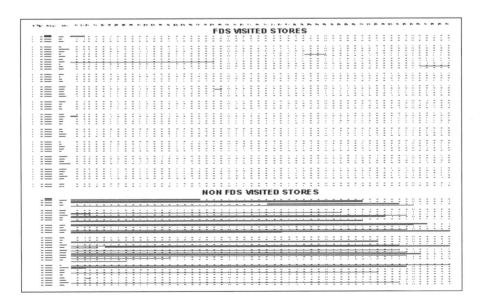

Figure 14.1 Visited vs non-visited stores

The results are very clear: a customer cannot purchase if the product is out of stock.

In a piece of research like this the client can clearly see the effects on one of the product ranges if there are no field visits, the potential lost sales are clearly high.

Value for money

The false economy of reducing staff pay levels

Quite rightly, everyone likes to be given a keen price for the work they commission. With FM, while it depends on the job, generally speaking between 80 per cent and 90 per cent of a costing will be for the staff-related issues. Therefore, if you ask for a reduction in price, it will almost certainly impact on staff pay and this may jeopardize the quality of the work to be done or reduce staff levels.

To be sure you have a keen price, ask for an open costing, then look to see where you think savings can be made and discuss this with the FM company. There is a balance to be found. There are large corporations that every FM company wants to see on its client list. Some companies will go to any length to win work from them, and this includes lower pricing. After all it is a brave FM company that turns down a prestigious named client. The experience at FDS is that not being paid a decent rate for a job means that the FM company makes no money, the account handlers are demotivated, and solid and sound delivery seldom follows. Reduction of pay to the field can have the same effect; these people know their worth – and quite rightly.

Loyalty and regular work from the staff is an important aspect of driving the sales forward in the ongoing development of the ROI model. It is a fact that staff working for the few companies who pay less will drop that company immediately there is work from a better paid source and the required consistency will be missing. Most companies are fair and understand this situation – do not be one of the ones that does not.

Equally, the failure of an FM exercise, particularly with a client new to the industry, can lead to the client's total disillusionment about FM, and a long time before that client will come back. Management staff in an FM company should never take the price below what they feel is correct; if you pay low wages the job will not receive the commitment from the field and the job will fall down; most clients should be aware of this. Mutually beneficial contracts are the most successful.

When a task is conducted where ROI is monitored and evaluated it is easy to see what is being achieved, and the quality of the work and the returns driven to the bottom line will define the success.

The above should give an insight about the objectives that will drive the ROI model which your FM agency will implement once it is agreed.

See also Chapter 16, where the costs of staff churn are discussed, as well as SLAs and KPIs.

Summary

The FM industry uses ROI to mean the marginal increased contribution generated with the entire costs of the campaign deducted. This measurement is complex (as a number of factors build into the ROI model) but it is not complicated in that it is a straightforward calculation. ROI is not intended to meet any accountancy criteria, but it offers the client a dynamic and measurable way of understanding what his expenditure on FM has achieved for the company and brand in terms of profit. The return can be awesome. The difficulty in demonstrating this in this book is obtaining figures, overcoming the secretiveness and client confidentially from within the industry. The key factor is perhaps how much of a multiplier is spending money on FM worth? Is raising sales by a factor of near times four beneficial? Or an uplift in sales by 20 per cent over a year? Or a seven-figure sum increase in a year just by applying merchandising? An alternative way is perhaps to examine who is using FM (through the methods described in the Preface) just as, say, trying to examine the effectiveness of sales promotion against advertising (where perhaps a measure of relative success is obtained by noting that three times as much is spent on the former than the latter in the UK. Can all those people be wrong?).

Finally, this chapter notes that like everything in life you get what you pay for. Cut the FM budget too drastically and it impacts immediately on staff, which reduces face-to-face activity, which will affect ROI.

Self-study questions

14.1. List the fundamentals, also known as compliance, that can be used for KPIs which will contribute to the ROI model and assist in defining ROI.

14.2. What might be selected as ROI goals?

14.3. How do you measure market share gain?

(Answers can be found in the text.)

15 How to select an FM agency as a partner

Procurement and what to look for

In the beginning

The selection process

Typically a telephone call to an FM agency asks whether they are interested in a project. If the answer is 'yes', a brief is sent across. On receipt of the brief, the FM agency produces a submission with costings. This is compared with other competitor submissions and a shortlist is drawn up. Then two or three FM agencies are interviewed. There may be further activity but from all this an FM agency is selected. That is what this chapter describes – how the FM agency is procured. It starts with the client producing a brief to send out to a number of agencies. The better the brief the better the submissions.

There are occasions when the client decides to see several agencies, where they present their credentials, without knowing what the brief is. This means the client may have selected people the client felt he or she could work with and who had the experience **before** sending out the brief. In essence, this makes little difference to the process described here.

Summary of actions for a client

- Write a comprehensive brief – see the example later in this chapter.
- Select a few FM agencies to respond to this brief (for example, six) in writing. Visit www.dma.org.uk to obtain a list of all the FM companies that are members of the FMC. These are all bona fide FM companies

that have signed up to the codes of conduct of the DMA and the best practice guidelines set out by the FMC.

- Read the submissions and select all those agencies you want to come to present to you (at this point drop one or two if they do not seem up to the mark).
- Spend time meeting the agencies you want to meet. Allow about one and a half hours for each agency. Tip – don't try to cram them all in one day, you will be too tired to think. Ask to see a client list. Try to get a feel for what each agency did for clients. At this point you can also ask for client referrals, so that you can speak to some of the agencies' current clients.
- Shortlist two or three agencies, perhaps asking them for more detail, or make your selection based on who you believe will deliver the best job.
- Bear in mind that you will need to work with these people, so select a team that you think will work with you, and with whom you could work, as any significant differences might not help communication in the future.

An overview of procurement

Procurement in general

If you intend to do this on a large scale as a client, there is undoubtedly a need for a procurement department to analyse and assess the pitch documents tendered, and pull them to pieces and rebuild them. FM agencies should be put through their paces and made to think and compete.

Case study: Pitching success

One agency, as an example, has been through a couple of long, gruelling pitches which they won and on both occasions the client department that held the budget (and ultimately had to work with the FM agency) made the final choice. On both occasions the FM agency was not the cheapest option. The two pitches put the FM agency 'through the mill' but the FM agency believe the client got the best out of their staff and ultimately the client felt it had made the decision it felt was best for the business and which was a rewarding experience for the FM agency too.

There is always also the real problem of comparing like with like, which is where an experienced procurement department helps. Instances where this does not happen can be frustrating for the FM agency. Where a less comprehensive service is not recognized by the client and its procurement department, unsurprisingly it costs less. The fact that the service was less comprehensive was not what the client's management wanted but they did not recognize the difference between two services being compared and were disappointed at the end of their campaign. Failure of an FM project or campaign reflects very badly on the industry. This can be avoided by bringing in several agencies to present to the same group of people. Then the differences between them will be more clearly understood. Price should never be the 'be all and end all', particularly with FM, where the dominating factors are delivery and paying people.

The pitch in general

The FM agency staff should have done their homework and know the key persons in your client team. They should ensure that they present answers that your key persons would demand without having to call for them. They should have a feel for your business. They should not present organigrams but match people from their FM teams to your task with the particular skills you require to complete your project. They should start with a picture of your problem as they see it – as outlined in Chapter 12. They should give a clear indication of how they would tackle the problem with a project in a bespoke and innovative way – not simply applying template solutions that they have cobbled together from previous client work. They should move on to describe typically the kind of profit you might expect and what revenue expenditure (cost) would be required to achieve what ROI.

Extract yardsticks from each team that is pitching, from which you can then measure the other solutions being offered. For the first team you should always ask them to be on standby for some additional questions at the end as a result of hearing the later pitches.

Timing

The procurement process can be very drawn out and ponderous (a year is not unusual) and it takes a phenomenal amount of time and cost from the FM agency, and carries huge amounts of frustration when the costs from different companies who have quoted for very different levels of services and support are compared.

It is very likely that the time it takes is the biggest single frustration for both the client and the FM agency. A year is a long time for a client to put new plans on hold until the client has the person to do the job selected, let alone up and running; and a year is a long time for an FM agency to spend several days every month to reproduce proposal after proposal according to the latest template drawn up by procurement, as they strive to compare bananas and tomatoes. This is why it is important to all, that the best available brief is prepared. Everyone benefits.

Once the decision is made

Let all the FM agencies know why they succeeded or did not succeed. In such a relatively small industry it is most helpful, particularly as you will probably be asking the company to pitch again. It should also sharpen up the company's presentations for the future – again saving everyone's time. Just as the better the brief the better the result; the better the presentation if the FM agency knows what you expect.

The brief

Basics

Some sections of the brief just give your details as the client, contact information and a deadline; the outline timescale for the proposed project and other related factors affecting the timescale; and details of reporting, communicating and administration.

The project as a proposal

The more information you can give about the project and the activities you see as part of the project the better. The objective and the outcome you would like to achieve in terms of product or service or brand are key. Also important is whether the activity is short term, ongoing or a mix of the two. The number of outlets, the FM disciplines you foresee using, and frequency and length of visits will give an idea of the scale of the project. Include any special need of the FM team. If some of the information you are giving is confidential, then obtain a signed non-disclosure agreement (NDA) from the FM agency before you send the brief.

You should also supply information on materials you have available, distribution (who handles what how often) and the nature of the call file and its availability.

A template for a brief, which is not conclusive, appears below.

Tips for commissioning an FM agency

Use FM expertise in drawing up the brief

FM brief for prospective clients

Client contact information			
Company name			
Company address			
Company telephone		Company fax	
Company website			
Contact name			
Contact job title			
Contact telephone		Contact mobile	
Contact e-mail			
By when would you like a response to this brief?			

The brief			
1.1	Describe in outline the activity to be undertaken		
1.2	What product(s) or service(s) are involved?		
1.3	What is the objective of the activity?		
1.4	What is the expected outcome?		
1.5	What level of conversion rate do you anticipate?		
1.6	Are sales and communication materials available for use by the field team?	Materials Available?	If YES go to 1.7 If NO go to 1.8
1.7	If YES to 1.6 what are the materials? e.g. contracts, order forms, planograms.		

Figure 15.1 Example brief

1.8	Is it a sales campaign?	Sales Campaign?	
1.9	Is it a one-off visit or ongoing?	Type of visit?	
1.10	What is the required frequency of visit?		If variable go to 1.11
1.11	If variable frequency state how many at each call rate		
1.12	What is your estimate of time to complete the activity at each location?		
1.13	How many locations are there?		
1.14	Would you like to hold a face-to-face briefing for the field team?	Face to Face Briefing?	
1.15	Are the field team required to have any specific qualifications?	Qualifications?	If YES go to 1.16 If NO go to 1.17
1.16	If YES what are the requirements?		
1.17	Are the team required to have any specific training?	Training?	If YES go to 1.18 If NO go to 2.1
1.18	If YES what are the requirements?		

Timescale			
2.1	When would you like this activity to go live?		Format DD/MM/YY
2.2	When would you like this activity to be completed?		Format DD/MM/YY
2.3	Other issues to consider in regards to this timescale:		

Figure 15.1 continued

The call file			
3.1	Are you able to supply a database of calls?	Database Supplied?	If YES go to 3.2 If NO go to 3.4
3.2	If a call file is supplied how many locations are to be visited?		
3.3	If a call file is supplied is a postcode breakdown of calls available?	Postcode Breakdown?	If YES please supply If NO go to 3.5
3.4	If a call file is not supplied how many calls are you hoping to receive?		
3.5	If a postcode breakdown of calls is not available which postcode areas do you wish to cover?		
3.6	Are you able to estimate how many calls are within the M25, Northern Ireland and any offshore islands e.g. Isle of Man or Channel Islands?	Call Source?	M25
			N. Ireland
			Offshore

Reporting procedures		
4.1	What information would you like back about the activity?	
4.2	How often would you like this information?	Reporting Frequency?
4.3	If other please state	
4.4	How would you like to receive this information? e.g. post, fax, e-mail, web-portal on the agency website?	Reporting Media?
4.5	If other please state	

Figure 15.1 continued

Distribution			
5.1	Does the activity require the agency to handle and distribute literature, POS or samples?	Material distribution?	If YES go to 5.2
5.2	If so what, how often, and what is the typical consignment size/weight?		

What to do now
Send this form to your chosen field marketing agency. If you haven't selected one yet you can see a full list of our field marketing members at www.dma.org.uk/Directory.

Figure 15.1 continued

Above all involve someone with FM expertise early in the development stages of the brief. If you have something about which you are unsure then ask one of the people in an FM agency you intend to ask to pitch. It will give the agency staff something to think about. They will advise what can be achieved, and how best to overcome any obstacles that might be presented. Experience shows several instances where the client has contrived a wonderful activity about which his entire board have been convinced, only to discover that parts of it were impossible. By including FM expertise at the beginning you will manage expectations by creating an activity that will work.

Have clear objectives

Be clear about your objectives and be sure that everyone understands them and has bought into them. This includes the FM agencies that are pitching and the one you select (that will provide the people responsible for delivering your objectives).

Timings are critical

Think carefully about what has to be done when. Use FM agency advice on timings. Once set, timings will need to be rigidly adhered to.

Try to think in advance of likely questions and answer them in the brief

All FM activities are individual, and designed to meet the client's requirements, remember this, think ahead and provide answers for possible questions related to the brief, even for the simplest task. Costs will vary according to the type of work, the staff skills required, the level of training needed, location and the logistics involved, so do not expect an FM company to have a fixed rate card.

Do not expect immediacy

Projects and campaigns do take some time to set up, and always remember that the best staff are not sitting waiting for your job to come in tomorrow! So, unless there is a crisis, allow a few weeks to get a project up and running.

Crisis projects

In a crisis, for example when items need removing from shelves, an FM company is best placed to assist: they have the systems and staff in place to be up and running quickly, and will always work as hard and fast as possible to protect the client, by dealing with the issues as soon as possible. In crisis management where there are instances of removing food from shelves, recalling incorrectly labelled products and other such problems can be dealt with. Conducting an exercise at speed to deal with a crisis might mean that some of the planning will not be 100 per cent spot on. Be prepared for this.

Partnership

Above all, the client and the FM company will have the same objectives and the same desire to achieve and succeed, therefore **they should work as partners to help each other to achieve the common goals.** The job as field marketers is to make clients look successful, then the FM company looks and is successful too.

Auction procurement and FM

Internet auction

You may come across a procurement process called an internet auction. This was common for a time but probably does not produce the best agency for the job, merely the one that is good at internet auctions. Generally, price is king in an auction, whereas what you are looking for as a client is a partner and trusted friend to whom you intend to outsource your sales function. In FM we are often dealing with the handling of relationships between a client and the client's customer, this is not a commodity and therefore is a trickier item to bid for or against.

An auction is suited to the purchase of commodities, say 2,000 ballpoint pens, or a fleet of cars, both a classic case for an auction, after all ballpoint pens are just that, whereas personalities and relationships are subjective, and do not sit easily within a procurement exercise. Auctions would be valid if it were a purely objective exercise.

The auction itself is conducted after several FM agencies have been given a brief, which has been answered carefully and full costs given. All of the selected FM agencies are then asked to log on at a specific time. On the screen are the costs for each section of the brief from each agency, although no agency is identified. Each is given a number or a letter of the alphabet as identification. Looking at the screen, you know which company is yours, but you do not know who the others are, although you can see their costs.

The client's procurement team then ask you to give your best price on that specific section of the proposal, and everyone inputs this information; you see what the others are putting in and you have to make your decisions as to whether you drop your prices to match or beat one of the other 'contestants'. The clear aim is to drive the price down.

Obviously, as for any business, FM companies have a duty to their staff and their owners to be commercial and make a profit, but as the margins are pushed down it is very scary to see what is happening on screen, and although you want the business, you have to maintain the integrity of the proposal.

As previously mentioned, this type of exercise cannot account for the personalities and rapport that the client will need with their chosen agency. This type of exercise is not suited to brand building campaigns. Nor does this type of exercise acknowledge that up to 90 per cent of a campaign is made up of staff-related issues, and if the price goes down too far, wages are affected, and the quality of staff and retention of staff could be affected in this scenario – an argument rehearsed and rejected earlier.

Going through an internet auction, although very challenging, is nerve-racking for an FM agency. For the reasons of personalities and different ways of working and the differing picture that FM companies will each give on the same project or campaign, an internet auction has the potential to be self-defeating, and both procurement departments and FM companies need to be very careful. We would hope that the internet auction is now recognized as not delivering the best FM company for any clients' projects.

Higher standards

There are of course many very positive procurement exercises which are handled very well, and allow the difference in agency price, attitude, ability, experience and personality to be showcased. In this environment, clients will understand what they are getting for their money, and will choose an agency that they feel they can work with, and that will deliver the results within the costs agreed.

FMC accreditation

The FMC has developed an accreditation scheme, which applies a very stringent test of compliance, processes and systems with an accredited member and will raise the standards in FM even higher than previously. In 2007 this scheme is being assessed by CIPS (Chartered Institute of Purchasing and Supply), and it is hoped that the scheme will meet their approval and be recommended to their members. Client FM users are also being asked to input to the scheme, so that it is robust. Many clients are now insisting on FMC membership for their appointed agency – a move which is pleasing, as this will help to drive up the standards in the industry,

The FMC is also working on the development of qualifications in the FM arena, and it is hoped these will be available in a year or so. To check on this development, contact the DMA at www.dma.org.uk.

Summary

The objective here is to obtain an FM agency as a partner – one with whom you are comfortable sharing your commercial secrets and to whom you have the confidence to outsource all or a part of the sales function. The brief is the initial means of communicating and establishing clearly your objectives for FM in the minds of the FM teams in the agencies you have selected to pitch for your task. The better the brief the more likely the requirement will be understood. An example template for a brief is included in the text. Asking FMC accredited FM agencies to pitch will certainly be an excellent start to making the right choice.

Self-study questions

15.1.   What would you expect the stages of the procurement process for an FM agency to be? As an exercise how might that be modified for your own company?

15.2.   Decide on the FM activities you believe your company should outsource. What should the brief that you will send out to a number of FM agencies contain?

15.3.   What are three tips for commissioning an FM agency that you think are the most important?

(Answers can be found in the text.)

16 Maximizing the FM budget

Obtaining the best bang for your buck

This chapter is about managing the FM budgets and not necessarily cutting them.

Principles behind maximizing the FM budget

Bear in mind that FM is all about using people – people who can communicate, explain, negotiate and influence. This puts FM apart from any other marketing tool, so aim to use this flexibility and range of attributes to its full.

Consider the main objectives of a project or campaign and then consider what else could be done at the same time to add value. An FM specialist will be able to advise on what is possible and will, wherever possible, encourage the best use of the budget by adding this value.

The disciplines within FM are seldom carried out in isolation; frequently several disciplines are combined to achieve the best brand development and to maximize the value of the face-to-face contact. Such combinations, with thought and careful briefing, can save some duplication of effort and thus save cost.

It starts with procurement and the plan

The procurement process is the one that sets the parameters for the work. Chapter 15 goes into detail on this process, but it is worth repeating that up to 90 per cent of a budget is spent on staff-related issues. Questioning and considering how staff are proposed to be used should be applied to every element of the brief and the pitch during the procurement process. When the plan is being written, the same rigour should be applied to every task. This will optimize the use of staff. Consider what risk is incurred by reducing the calibre of staff, the level of staff, and the application of staff. Remember the example in Chapter 14 of removing merchandising. You get what you pay for, is the FM maxim. Think from the task point of view and the likely potential return and profit it generates. Reducing the resource committed to a task will not only reduce cost and consequent profit but may mean that the task fails and then there is no return. Remember too the motivation element. There is a point at which driving the price down will mean cuts to the wages paid to the staff. The human being has well-known capabilities and tasks should always be considered within that performance envelope.

The self-recognized value of FM staff

FM staff know their worth, and the best people will not work for the lower wages, and those who will may not stick with the work if they are offered a better position. This leads to staff churn, which is expensive in its own right, as the subsequent recruitment and training have a cost, let alone the fact that a territory may be uncovered for a period of time while a new person is found. In the office, working on a contract with very poor margins will not motivate the account team. There is a balance to be struck here, and it should be understood that it would not benefit a campaign if the price were driven down too far. To maximize a budget, reducing staff pay is not a recommended way forward. The effects of staff churn are covered in the next section.

Motivating the FM agency

Working with your FM agency

There is no doubt that working with your FM agency in a planned and agreed manner will save time, effort and budget. Allow time for the critical element of planning – the more time there is to plan, the better the results.

An FM agency that is treated as a partner will be motivated to respond. Outsourcing the sales function – the key to revenue generation – deserves high level and probably daily communication and a close relationship.

The FMC *Users' Guide to Field Marketing* (see www.dma.org.uk) states:

The client is best served when they:

- Involve the FM company at an early stage
- [Have] one client/Director voice, clear about his [or her] objectives
- Agree the critical timing issues
- Adhere to the critical timing.

The field marketing company will then:

- Achieve the best financial results for the client
- Ensure the objectives and processes are realistic, based on their past experience
- Advise the client on critical timing
- Give advice on added benefits of including other activities that extend the value of any project undertaken
- Implement the exercise according to the critical timing previously agreed
- Audit the results
- Devise the relevant reporting to meet the client's requirements.

Above all the client and the field marketing company should work as a partnership; after all they have one common aim – that the exercise should achieve the very best results possible.

Staff-related motivation – incentives

Maximize the budget by having well-motivated, keen staff working on a campaign; this will produce much better results.

Earlier in the book risk and reward are mentioned as a way of sharing the exposure of an activity (see Chapter 4). This can be truly motivational if the reward aspect is not forgotten. Provide incentives for the FM staff and some return for the agency for achieving targets, and stretch targets.

Staff churn

Staff churn has a cost. If staff churn is monitored and kept low, then costs are saved. The FM company should be constantly reviewing its recruitment plans so that the calibre of the staff recruited is improved, and that improvement is maintained.

Remember, every time there is a need to recruit:

- interviews have to be conducted;
- training has to be given to the newly appointed member of staff;
- the new member of staff has to 'get up to speed' before he or she is working most effectively;
- the territory he or she was recruited for may have been empty for a while and there will have been lost opportunities.

Case study: Example of staff churn

One agency found that by reviewing and varying the staff recruitment for one campaign that:

- Five area managers each had 8 per cent of time saved inducting new starters.
- Field service executives (FSEs) spent 38 per cent less time on training days.
- More time was spent in calls by the FSEs.
- More time was spent by area managers on field accompaniments and development of the FSEs.

Source: FDS

And all the above points have a cost attached to them.

The staff churn is always the lowest when the staff are clear in what they have to achieve, are well trained and managed, so that they have the skills to achieve. They also need to be motivated and work well within their team, area or division with praise and a reward being given when it is due.

SLAs

Both the client and the FM agency should sign an SLA. An SLA makes the whole project or campaign more efficient and effective as it details the responsibilities for both parties and creates the standards to which everyone should adhere. This also has the effect of minimizing extra costs as each party sticks to the timelines and responsibilities that are in the SLA.

Typical SLA

The topics to be included might include (although not exclusively, as all projects will vary):

- general:
  - length of contract;
  - method of dealing with extra costs should they occur outside the budget;
  - confidentiality (both ways);
  - action points (to be done at the correct time by both parties);
- service specification:
  - operational detail;
  - call activity;
- quality control:
  - how quality will be monitored and assessed;
  - communication (such as an agreement that both parties answer communications within fixed periods, for example e-mail within 3 days, letters within 5 days);
- liabilities: who is liable for what (this will vary from one contract to the next);
- head office support: defining what this is, level of support and from whom;
- reporting requirements: clarifying what the client wants, and what the FM company must deliver;
- KPI tracking: explaining how this will be done, when and noting the agreed review period;
- scheduled meetings and reviews: these are included in the SLA for clarity;
- costs (as applicable to the exercise).

As SLAs are written and agreed by both parties they often have the effect of ironing out a few misconceptions between the parties, so that by the time they are signed there is greater clarity.

KPIs

Typical KPIs

KPIs are the means of driving sales and results as well as contributing to the measurement of ROI. KPIs will be given at all levels of a campaign, for example imagine a sales drive where the three levels involved are the field sales executive (FSE), area sales manager (ASM) and the head office account team and their director (in the category called 'the company' in the examples below). The following are only examples, and this will vary from one campaign to another, but this should set the scene.

KPIs for an FSE:

- strike rate – number of calls made a day;
- sales made – number or value of sales made;
- distribution points achieved – number of new facings or secondary displays achieved in the stores visited, or the number of new stores added to the database via cold canvas (and sales or facings made to these stores too).

KPIs for an ASM:

- ensuring that all their FSEs are achieving all FSE KPIs as detailed above;
- staff churn – ie keeping staff leaving to a minimum.

KPIs for the company are to ensure that:

- FSEs and ASMs are all achieving their KPIs;
- all the account team are also achieving their KPIs regarding reports being on time, certain administrative functions being achieved for the client on time;
- quality checks are all being implemented and corrective action taken when necessary;
- many more activities are being completed, depending on the task in hand.

If the KPIs are achieved, the staff are all rewarded and targets are met. The results of the KPIs being fed into the ROI model, will be a large part of proving the level of ROI in the campaign.

Creativity

Creative thinking to maximize the budget

Using some creativity in thought and concept of the project or campaign will help to make the most of the budget and achieve the best results for that project or campaign.

Of course this creative thinking needs to be translated into delivery in the field, and this will be achieved by the FM company having its best practice in place, so that each step of the campaign is correctly implemented, from planning, training and management through to the results, analysis and the final report. Always be sure that you are encouraging the best use of the people, the brand ambassadors, the influencers, maximizing the opportunities for success, and making the most of the FM budget.

Making the most of the tools available

There are several tools that an FM company will have to help make the most of the budget. They include:

- Journey planning (see Chapter 11). This will plan the visits to be made using the least mileage and time, thus saving costs.
- Call grading (see Chapter 5). This will mean the correct frequency of call to the outlets to make the most of the personnel time.
- KPIs. KPIs in place so that the staff all work to achieve the standards required, and achieving the KPIs should give them a benefit as part of the risk and reward which is common in FM (see example of KPIs above).
- Staff to management ratio. This needs to be sufficient to get the work completed accurately, on time and enthusiastically and to get the best results but not overweighted, which will increase costs. This is a point for discussion and consideration with your FM partner.
- ROI monitoring (see Chapter 14). This will monitor the campaign to be sure it is on track, and working for both the client and the FM agency.
- Correct tools and technology for the job. This is important as it helps the staff to be efficient in the execution of their work; they will need such items as presenters, uniforms, cars, sales aids, appropriate IT resource (laptops or PDAs), store information, as appropriate. The more efficient the staff, the better the results in terms of calls per day, sales made, etc.
- Correct personnel development. Provide job descriptions for the staff and set IiP-based work objectives. Arrange accompaniments in the field from the management team, and have regular appraisals for each individual, so that all staff learn more, gain confidence and improve their performance and their results.
- Multi-disciplined calls. Make the call multi-disciplined if this is sensible. When merchandisers go into stores to place POS material, they could also sell in some product, conduct an audit and/or train the in-store staff to the product's features and benefits, thus maximizing the in-store time to achieve more from the call.

Creative design work for a campaign

The client, its advertising agency or its sales promotion agency often generates the creative work for a campaign, and for traditional FM work, the POS materials are most usually designed by the client's in-house design agency. For experiential work this is not usually the case, and many experiential exercises will have been developed entirely by the experiential agency. While there is no regular pattern, it is important to be aware that agencies can supply the creative work if required to do so.

Examples of maximizing a campaign

Some examples of how to get the most out of a project or campaign are given here, where doing more than might have been initially considered will add value to the exercise.

Example 1: A CRM campaign

Brief

To develop and enhance the contact that a client has with its customer – a retailer – and to raise profile for the brand with that customer.

The visit

The visit to the customer might include any number of elements forming an amalgamation of many disciplines. For example:

- merchandising to place POS material;
- training for the counter staff so that they know the features and benefits of the product or service and can make sales;
- auditing the stock levels to ensure that they will meet the increase in demand;
- completing a transfer order to replenish the stock if necessary;
- selling in a reward scheme to the manager, or explaining the profit margins on the product, telling the manager about a new advertising campaign – in fact anything that will encourage and help him to stock the product, sell it and make a profit;
- a meeting with the manager or owner to establish a point of contact, and over time develop a relationship with him or her so that the product receives care and attention;

- recording the data and comments from the visit so that this can be built upon during the next visit, and ensuring this information is available on the web that same day, so that the client can see the effect of the call and react as necessary.

In this way the CRM contact is multi-faceted and makes the best use of the call, and leaves the outlet in readiness to maximize sales.

Example 2: A sales drive in independent grocery stores

Brief

To sell in product to the independent stores to improve distribution and sales.

The visit

The visit might include:

- van or car sales selling in a special offer of the brand;
- merchandising a shelf in store, placing the product on a visible shelf, with a shelf talker and other POS material;
- training the manager or owner to the profit margins of the product and the features and benefits;
- supporting the chosen wholesaler from whom he or she can purchase repeat product;
- auditing the shop for future campaigns;
- downloading the results to the web-based report;
- category advice to increase sales.

Again the sell-in is enhanced by adding the elements that will help both the retailer and the brand by merchandising and training in the store, and also by recording the outlet's details, so that future contact can be relevant.

Example 3: Audit to evaluate standards of product presentation and service

The brief

To visit a number of public houses to assess the standards of pouring and presentation of a drinks product, so that the consumer receives it at its best.

The visit

The visit might include:

- making a mystery call to purchase the drink and observe the service;
- scoring the results against strict objective criteria to assess the positive and negative points;
- revealing the result to the bartender;
- training the bar personnel if they failed on the correct methods, what to do and why;
- congratulating and offering a winning outlet the staff's reward;
- selling in that the outlet will be mystery shopped again, and staff might win prizes if they are found to have improved;
- checking sales or stocks of the product and taking a transfer order;
- collecting the data about the outlet and/or the visit and using this in the report of the results for the client's records, and possibly for future work.

This exercise again takes the call to a new level by including several steps to the call that will make the best use of the in-call time, and the budget.

Summary

Making the best use of the budget refers to optimizing the skills, time and talents of the FM staff as they are the principal area of spend. Minimizing staff churn reduces the time spent managing and training new staff. Motivating and providing incentives for the FM agency, following all the best management of people principles, will encourage their staff to go the extra mile. Using SLAs will help define responsibilities and the standards expected. Selection of appropriate KPIs will also be an incentive, especially when the KPI targets are met and rewarded. As in any people business, concern for people will pay dividends.

Self-study questions

16.1. What does an SLA contain?
16.2. What is the impact of staff churn?
16.3. What are typical KPIs that might be used for a field sales executive?

(Answers can be found in the text.)

17 The law, staff pay, health and safety

In this chapter it is not possible to cover all the points relevant in this complex area, as it is always evolving and changing. Topics are well documented elsewhere. However, the highlights are here that relate to FM, so that you can understand some of the considerations you should have when engaging in FM activity. FM companies will have their own HR specialists to check that all they do is correct, or you can use your own HR specialist or legal specialist to check the detail. This chapter is only to guide you to the areas in which you should be interested, further information in this ever-changing area will be crucial.

The critical importance of such subjects as employment law, insurance and health and safety must be stressed, as these are the areas where incorrect application could lead to injury, illegality and subsequently significant costs at any court or tribunal hearing. Any FM company you use should be compliant in terms of these areas, and the best way to be sure of this is to use an FM company that is a member of the FMC as they will have been examined and tested as compliant.

Codes of practice and best practice guidelines

Both of these are very important in ensuring that work is done ethically and correctly as well as being conducted in the best interests of the brand.

Members of the FMC sign up to the codes of practice for the DMA and also adhere to the very comprehensive best practice guidelines, written by the FMC, which apply specifically to FM. A register of all the FM companies that have signed up to the codes of practice and adhere to the FMC best practice guidelines can be found on the DMA website at www.dma.org.uk.

To read the FMC best practice guidelines take the following steps:

Access www.dma.org.uk → Councils and Committees → Field Marketing → Best Practice

Reading these documents will help you to understand what the expectation should be and help with your views and deliberations. The documents are available to purchase from the same website.

Employment law

With the laws from Europe becoming increasingly complicated, it is crucial that an FM company is fully conversant with the detail. People will take advice in different ways, and members of the FMC do have an employment lawyer at the DMA on whom they can call for free advice. It is understood that EU law on employment now covers anyone who works more than 10 hours per year for a company. At the same time, agency law affects even casual workers who might be employed by an FM company. This is all explained below in the type of contracts for employees – see the bullet point below on tactical field workers.

Some companies will pay an annual fee to a group of employment lawyers so that they have access to advice around the clock. They will also purchase indemnity insurance to cover costs of employment claims and provision of third parties to resolve claims at employment tribunal. This retained advice offers help in the preparation of contracts, employee handbooks, and in staff development, training and the setting up of an HR department, all of which is important, as there are several different types of employee in a typical FM company, including:

- Full-time office staff (working on employment contracts with no definite end date).
- Part-time office staff (as above, but employed to work less than the standard hours detailed in the full-time contract).
- Full-time field staff (with terms and conditions related to the project – known as a project contract – which will cease when the project ends). If

these employees have more than one year's service with the company, a redundancy situation would arise when the project contract ends and the redundancy procedure should be followed.

- Part-time field staff (ie working a fixed number of days a week or month) (as field staff above, but working to reduced hours).
- Tactical field workers engaged as and when needed, ranging from every week on differing activities to only a few days a year. These are casual workers who are not employed, but for legal purposes would be determined 'workers'. They are usually given a casual agreement whereby they are offered work on an 'as and when' basis. We are not legally obliged to offer them work and they are not legally obliged to accept the work. These workers are very rarely covered under any indemnity insurance as they are not employees and not covered by a contract of employment.
- Zero hours contract workers, whereby no hours are guaranteed but the person is an employee and has a contract of employment.

Each level of employee requires appropriate contracts and terms of employment or engagement.

Additionally, providing the FM company sticks to the instructions from the retained lawyers, the FM company is indemnified against any actions that might be taken and damages that might be paid out. Payments are not made for health and safety or tactical workers in most cases, as health and safety issues come under civil or criminal law and tactical workers are not employees.

This is a complex area, which is continually changing, and any user of FM should be aware that all employment processes are correct at all times. This is particularly important for a client who needs the reassurance that this is all taken care of legally on his or her behalf.

Staff pay

Legal payment of staff (PAYE and schedule D)

Field staff in FM are paid in two ways: under the PAYE scheme or under Schedule D (for the self-employed).

Within the Schedule D arena, there are two types of company: an arbitrary set up or a revenue approved company. This matter was investigated very carefully by the FMC, and the result was that the FMC will have no association with the arbitrary company, but will admit a revenue approved company to membership.

A revenue approved company will run company processes in a very different way from a more usual PAYE paying company, and providing these processes are adhered to, there is no risk to the client should anything go wrong. If the rules are not adhered to, then the revenue approved operator runs the risk of a double jeopardy whereby he or she will have to pay National Insurance to the HM Revenue & Customs as well as leaving himself or herself liable to employment law claims from the company's self-employed staff, (a significant risk if processes and rules are not kept.)

Many agencies operating Schedule D are not revenue approved. The risk to the client and the reputation of his or her brand is severely at risk if the client chooses to use one of these companies. It cannot be recommended.

The vast majority of FM companies employ staff on a PAYE basis, this means they have to pay National Insurance and allow for pay for holidays, sickness, maternity, paternity, etc as appropriate. This type of employment is what most of us in the UK understand.

The client needs to be sure that all staff are paid legally, as any public repercussions could damage the brand. Again, FMC members are audited on this subject, and using an FMC member will give the client reassurance.

Late payment

FM companies have suffered from clients being late to pay, and this puts real strain on the FM company's cash flow. Staff must be paid on time if they are to be loyal to the FM company and the client, and waiting to pay the staff until the client has paid the FM company is not acceptable. Nobody would dream of delaying pay to the office staff until the client had paid, so why should the field wait?

The worst offenders used to be (sorry to say) the sales promotion (SP) agencies, who would commission work, pass it on to the client, and then not pay the FM company until weeks after they had been paid by the client. Frankly, FM companies prefer to work with the client direct, and nowadays this happens. In the past it was always the case that SP agencies marked up the FM work, and the only way they had of securing their mark-up was to make the FM company invoice them, and keep the client out of the loop. Nowadays, with open costings this does not occur, but we have known times when the SP agency earned more for themselves with their FM mark-up, than we, the FM agency, had earned fulfilling the entire task. This is not the case now, as far as I am aware.

In the past some clients have expected the FM company to bank roll their activities, so changes have been implemented. Now an FM company will negotiate monies up front to meet immediate costs, and in very large exercises will receive often a monthly payment in advance, with open reconciliation at the month end. This is a very common arrangement.

Staff will also require reimbursing for expenses, mileage and any other 'out of pocket' costs. This should also be dealt with promptly. All users of FM should have a fairly clear idea of what these out of pocket expenses will be, and these might well be a part of the up-front payments that will be made, so that the field staff can be reimbursed promptly.

Insurance

Every FM company will require several layers of insurance, including (although not exclusively) product and public liability, employers' liability, and professional indemnity. These are essential; indeed public liability insurance (of at least £10 million) is a standard requirement for working in most public places, such as shopping centres and railway concourses.

Public liability, employers liability and professional indemnity policies are fairly standard, but product liability insurance might vary in content. Product liability insurance should cover all the client's and the FM company's equipment (laptops, stands, uniforms samples, POS, etc) for both loss and damage, and note there would be an excess for valuable items such as alcohol and tobacco.

Contents insurance will cover items stored in FM warehouses and offices, and again, excess for alcohol and tobacco or similar will apply. Car insurance should be uplifted to include business use and goods in transit where applicable, as these are not automatically insured otherwise.

FDS hold Business Interruption Insurance, in case there is ever an issue of a delay to a client's work through an unexpected disaster, say death, fire or similar at the FM company.

Having legal defence costs insured is a comfort too.

It is only when things go wrong that anyone appreciates the value of insurance. See also www.businesslink.gov.uk/casestudies for a case study entitled 'Here's what I learned about contingency planning after a disaster'.

Health and safety

As with any well-run company, all companies will have a health and safety policy in operation in the offices and in the field. This will probably form part of their employee handbook as well as being signposted in the offices and highlighted in training sessions. Health and safety will be relevant, for example, when loading vehicles for ex-car sales, if selling tins of food or drink, picking up parcels and also for guidelines to prevent overloading vehicles.

As with any company, there is of course a duty of care for employers and employees. For employers, this is to provide a safe place of work and safe working practices. For FM this means providing staff and tactical workers with health and safety training, for example on lifting heavy goods.

Summary

This is a chapter designed to alert the reader that there are legal, health and safety, employment (HR) and insurance problems related to FM activities. As the situation changes with time, the contents of this chapter should be taken merely as a guide, a pointer to areas of concern rather than a definitive source. The FMC accredited FM agency will be up to speed on the latest requirements but help can also be obtained from the DMA website.

Self-study questions

17.1. What are the different ways in which FM staff are employed?
17.2. In what two ways are staff paid and in what two ways do agencies operate on pay?
17.3. For FM operations what insurance cover do you need to consider?

(Answers can be found in the text.)

18 FM practice in the international arena

There is a rise in interest in FM abroad in 2007, especially in Eastern Europe. The FM agencies that operate abroad are most wary of sharing any case studies or experience of FM activity on behalf of clients. However, as the change in customer behaviour spreads, specifically the move to internet purchasing, and the need for brand experience, astute businesses, especially those in retail, are anticipating the need for FM for the future. They are aware of FM but have not as yet put much into practice as the UK and other parts of Europe.

In Europe there are three main types of strategic contract:

- Where there is one client who issues one contract for the whole of Europe that one agency handles, for example Hewlett Packard.
- Where there is one client who appoints one agency to run the client's business, but that one agency will then recruit other agencies in Europe to fulfill the business. The client has one point of contact but across several agencies, for example Disney.
- Where there is one client who designs an activity for one country; the rest of Europe are told about the activity and what it should achieve, and the client managers for the other countries decide whether they wish to implement the campaign from their budgets or not, for example Mars.

For tactical campaigns an activity is designed, and this then rolls out to the other countries, but will need to be adapted to meet the laws, regulations and culture of the different countries; the promotion will have the same overall 'feel', but may well be operated differently.

When considering conducting an FM campaign in countries other than your own, you should bear the following in mind. Each country may well have different laws, different operational rules and a different culture; so what works in one country may well not succeed in another. An activity can be run in different countries that can have very similar objectives, a very similar look and feel and very similar results, but this should be checked out before the plans are too advanced, so that activities can be adapted to meet the local requirements. Even in Europe, for example, there are different languages, different laws and differing cultures. There are simple, basic differences too, for example the 2-litre Coca Cola bottle does not fit in Spanish fridges; a campaign that works in the UK might not work in the hotter, more languid Latin countries like Spain and Italy. In short, do not presume to have any FM expertise you can necessarily apply – use a local in-country FM expert.

Doing international FM business

For the client it is easier to have one point of contact for an international campaign for ease of communication and language, so to facilitate the implementation of an international campaign a few of the larger FM companies in the UK have a series of affiliated or owned partners through whom they can work. The client then communicates with his or her FM contact in the UK, for example, and that contact will coordinate the campaign through these partners in the other countries.

The overseas FM companies will then understand the objectives and operation of the campaign from their UK partners, and will adapt this, if necessary, to suit their country. Their costing and modus operandi will be made clear, and the client has the comfort of knowing that a specialist in each of the countries in question is dealing with their campaign.

One group, the European Field Marketing Partners (EFMP), selects their members to all fit certain criteria; members must be Independent, experienced in FM, and be known operators in their country with client references being sought. The owners of these agencies attend regular meetings and share best practice, thus there is a level of conformity and standards with such a group that might not otherwise exist. The EFMP insists on all members being FM specialists. EFMP can be found on www.efm-partners.com.

As FM is not fully developed in some countries, it can be the case that a more general marketing agency will conduct FM from time to time. Of course such an agency is local, the staff know the law, and while they are not FM specialists, many will understand what they have to achieve and can work towards doing this quite well, although it is safer if the task is not over-complicated. These general agencies may not have staff lists and profiling, and may not have the reporting tools of an FM company for example, but some can do a fair job despite FM not being their usual discipline. This is most likely in the developing countries.

There are global marketing groups such as Saatchi, WPP and Omnicom who have an international reach, and their overseas offices might well be able to advise on local FM agencies, if they cannot complete the work themselves. The DMA in the UK has affiliated Direct Marketing Associations throughout the world. www.dma.org/directory will give a full list of these. These DMA offices will be able to give advice and help. The DMA in the UK is the largest marketing trade association in Europe and in the world it is second only to the US DMA.

It is not possible to be specific on the international arena, as the countries are all different and laws are ever-changing. The key is to find FM specialists in the countries of your choice.

Case study: Demonstrating mobile phones at European airports

Objective

A large mobile phone company commissioned a UK FM company to carry out airport demonstrations for the launch of a new model. The activity ran for 14 days in 22 airports in the following countries: Austria, Denmark, Finland, France, Germany, Holland, Italy, Poland, Portugal, Spain, Sweden, Switzerland and the UK.

The objectives of the promotion were:

- To demonstrate the handset and digital camera and discuss their functions and benefits.
- To encourage travellers to purchase the products from their local outlets or airport tax-free shop.
- To collect business cards from interested passengers as potential sales leads.
- To distribute brochures.

Process

Staff experienced in the demonstration of high-end electronic goods were booked in the UK and in the other countries through the FM company's affiliated FM agencies.

Training was carried out in each country to optimize costs.

A prize of a mobile phone was offered as an incentive to the best-performing team.

Results

- The main interest in the products came from 35–55-year-old business travellers (who made up 55 per cent of the 58 per cent of the passenger profile classed as business travellers).
- Travellers were impressed with the many functions and uses of the phone and its weight and size. (The product was judged 'Excellent' by 36 per cent of respondents and 'Good' by 56 per cent).
- In two weeks, 14,000 business cards were collected.
- Almost half a million brochures were distributed at the airports (over 20,000 per airport).

The client was pleased with the increase in awareness of the products among an expertly targeted group across Europe. The client was also pleased with the quantity of literature distributed and level of expertise provided by field personnel that enabled its product to be handled by a large number of people.

Many recommendations were made to the client by the FM company in its final report. These include the inclusion of a worldwide product stockist list with the literature and more effort put in to adequate stock levels at airport shops. Many had neither item in stock. Of those that did, Stockholm sold its 20 phones on the first day, while Heathrow sold its three almost immediately.

Training of promotional personnel was carried out through the client's local offices but there was consistency in the product information imparted to the demonstrators, as a result of the brief being agreed in advance.

Lessons from the case study

Checking stocks in an airport is complicated by the issue of secure stock, some of it tax or duty free, and also security issues, but the main lesson from this is that despite checking the airports, the client was unable to influence the stock levels, which was a disappointment.

Case study: European-wide distribution of 'take ones'

Background

'Take ones' are the cardboard holders into which leaflets are placed, so that people can just 'take one'. These are placed where people are spending a bit of time waiting, such as queuing in a shop, waiting to be served in a bar or restaurant, in reception at offices, clubs, travel areas and so on.

'Take ones' for a pan-European campaign were prepared and the lead agency in Holland selected. The lead agency contacted the partners throughout Europe and sent out the brief and the staff training manual in English. These had to be translated in some countries, and the staff were trained for the campaign.

Additionally all the support material, although multi-lingual, had to have the local language on the holder, and made the distribution of the holders to the appropriate country tricky, as they all looked the same.

All the countries went live at about the same time, and the 'take ones' were all over Europe.

As 'take ones' had proven to be a profitable route to market, the simple placement of the containers and their leaflets produced excellent results, and the presence and market share for the client was impressively improved.

Summary

Remember that the rules may be different overseas. Many countries are very good at FM and offer a similar service to that in the UK, however, some countries do not, and this is where care should be taken. If the project is very difficult, be wary in countries where you may not be in touch with an FM specialist.

Coordinate the activity through one agency if you wish, but examine the costs from all the agencies and check what those costs cover, to avoid any hidden extras. Have a contingency fund, as well as the regular operational issues that might require contingency, you may need some translation (most countries operate in English, but some have more difficulty with this than others).

Check that the staff will be insured and paid by the local agency. (An accident getting into the press would be very damaging.)

The marketing for brands is often controlled on a continental basis, with each continent having autonomy on the work conducted, although this is not always the case. In Europe, some companies are aiming to work across the continent, but it is a fragmented continent in terms of language, culture, food and attitude – not a problem, for example, that the North American continent experiences to the same extent.

International FM came about for companies to achieve some consistency in their brand marketing, and perhaps to achieve some economies in terms of time and effort in the implementation across the different countries. It differs depending on whether FM companies are centralized or decentralized in their structures, but the nature of FM operating in different countries means that there are always cultural and legal factors to take into account.

Borderless FM disciplines work where there is a single international target audience. In most cases, international FM projects or campaigns go across multiple-countries, and vary in terms of timing and detail from country to country. Succeeding requires close attention to be paid to the behaviour and culture of each market in which you are promoting.

Self-study questions

18.1. What two differences can you think of between running a campaign in Germany and running the same campaign in Greece?

18.2. Why is it important to have specialist local knowledge?

18.3. Experience shows that limited product or brand availability has occurred in international FM. What additional activities would you operate in support of an FM campaign demonstrating a mobile phone at a number of international airports?

(Answers can be found in the text.)

19 Face-to-face sales – in-house

Sales in-house – a non-FM world

The face-to-face world that is bereft of FM

As explained in the Preface, this final chapter, for completeness, describes the in-house scene and how it might be improved – because, it too, is face-to-face. This chapter is put into this book as the general situation in the retail, B2B, B2C and B2P sectors is poor with regard to sales – there is an urgent need for improvement. There are reasons for this – cost, sales, staff churn, etc – but that does not excuse a near total lack of investment in sales staff training in marketing including sales as a generality. The start of this book describes the poor retail sector experience over winter 2006–2007. Logic would suggest that a reason may be the lack of sales training and this is important given the 2007 customer's need for face-to-face selling. Chapter 1 describes how the customer now seeks a relationship and recognition as a customer. Some retailers are reacting positively to this change in the customer, but they are few in number. This chapter hopes to address the problem of a lack of marketing, including sales training of in-house staff, which is found not only in retail but in the non-retail sectors too.

Remember the bottom level of the sales hierarchy are the shop or sales assistants and, until they have spent time with a company, they hardly receive much training. The investment in this training is costly, but the return could be handsome. For even the sales assistant is face-to-face.

Whether a business appreciates it or not the salesperson represents the brand, both of the outlet and those of the brands that are on sale. It is no longer enough to just be capable of processing an order once the decision to buy has been made. Nor can providing a 'happy' service, however courteous and customer-facing, really be defined as sales as this book considers it. A successful sale activity is putting an offer forward that persuades the customer of its value, then the offer is accepted by the customer. The same applies to services; bar and table staff in restaurants meet the same issue – a bit of advice on the menu or wine list is nowadays often sought, appreciated and taken up. The customer wants a relationship with the brand ambassadors whether they are in-house or outsourced. The DIY sheds are learning that proffering advice is welcomed too, but this is still only halfway to real selling which requires a close.

This chapter is not concerned with the process of simple order fulfilment: taking an item, wrapping it, entering the item into the company computer system through a bar code reader and then taking payment. That is not face-to-face sales, simply face-to-face service. The chapter is concerned with the pre-purchase decision that selects a better product, more products – the period of time when a salesperson can persuade a customer to buy.

Over the years, social custom and practice have required the consumer to make purchase selections on their own. In the supermarket, for years, we have arrived and trundled the trolley around making decisions on what to buy. But the world is moving on. The consumer wants a relationship. They want help with the decision taking. They want to be sold a product or service. They want to buy into a reasoned trusted sales argument to persuade and convince them they have made the correct choice for their purchase. In short, they seek a face-to-face sales experience.

Some suppliers have realized that just offering products to sample is not enough. Customers need and value the FM demonstrator alongside the sampling and demonstrating; or at experiential marketing, roadshows and events the presence of an FM team to take them through the experience; or FM staff offering highly targeted sales, particularly in places with high footfall, such as retail sheds, department stores and – wait for it – supermarkets. As consumers we like not just to sample, but to get into dialogue, to hear advice, so the retail experience becomes once again a beneficial, personally justifying and learning process for the customer. FM panders to it. Indeed, this book is full of advice on FM practices taken to the highest professional level – that of the field marketer. Outsourcing of sales is at last becoming more common and should now be a routine consideration of the board of any company. Chapter 10 describes how FM supports the training of in-house sales staff to a better level for some FM projects. So let us consider how just a small amount of in-house effort to train in-house staff might pay off. Such consideration will also demonstrate, if extrapolated, how using the professionals – an FM agency – and outsourcing the sales function, would be likely to really pay dividends.

One of the authors has in recent years trained his own clients (for example, one makes jewellery, another retail gifts) to spend time with their B2B customers (retail outlets) helping to train their B2B customers' in-house sales staff in selling their products to consumers. These clients do this because the return is really rewarding. More of their products are sold as a result. The outlets concerned are not just small outlets, but department stores such as John Lewis. In reality they are applying the ideas in Chapter 10 to a limited extent, like an FM agency does.

This chapter gives guidance towards improvement of the in-house operation rather than providing a total solution. This is because the variety of situations is too large. For a bespoke solution, a chartered marketer is required.

Here scenarios are considered as to how in-house sales staff could be trained in some small way to improve face-to-face situations in your business or a client business you supply, to increase sales and to improve your brand in customers' eyes, to the benefit of your bottom line. ROI really pays off in face-to-face situations as this book, and Chapter 14 in particular, describes.

Improving selling in-house

Sales staff need to learn about customers and why they buy. Underhill (see the 'Further information' section) wrote a book on the subject with all the reasoning based on research at the point of sale. He found that if people are offered a shopping basket they buy more. Mintel reports that up to 70 per cent of buying decisions are made at the point of purchase. So selling – which is persuading a customer to purchase – is a powerful skill to have. It should logically follow the preferred buying process and buying behaviour of your customers (touched on in Chapter 1).

The staff then need to know that the first words said are wasted, as human beings take a finite time to adjust their hearing and brain to a voice. So a greeting is appropriate and a non-threatening but indicating a potentially beneficial dialogue started, such as 'I see you are looking at ..., that is one of our best selling products'.

The buying process is shown in Table 19.1 in the first column and follows a customer's needs. For each element of the process a sales response is included and practical procedures that can be employed by the salesperson.

The buyer process should be translated for your sales staff as training in a sales process. The sales process varies according to the product or service. Customers buy a sofa and two chairs in quite a different way from the way they buy a jar of jam or pickles or a pair of socks.

The sales process can also be shown tabled (see Table 19.2). The first column shows the point a customer has reached in the process. The salesperson has to discover this by asking questions. At each stage of the process the salesperson has an objective and practical steps are given as to what to do at that stage. The sales process illustrated is generalized. The text is shortened in the table. For each product it can be tuned to match target groups of customers. Sales staff soon learn the sales process by heart.

By way of example, if a potential customer and his or her partner arrive to buy that sofa and two chairs then, if this is the first store they have visited, the sales staff need to realize they are unlikely to buy, especially if they do not know the brand. The sales process for a sofa and two chairs includes a search of a number of furniture outlets. But you can still do a lot to secure a sale in that situation even if you are the first outlet visited. All the features of the offer and brand values need to be put across but preferably as asides or responses to fact finding about the potential customers: 'What size sofa and two chairs can you fit in your room? Let me show you our range that match

Table 19.1 Responses to the buyer process elements

Buyer process – needs	Perfect response	Practical steps
Identify Define Specify	Your offer's six Cs match the buyer's needs	Find out Qualify Articulate the offer
Search	Buyer is fully aware of the offer and its benefits at the right moment	Marketing Make contact with matched offer message
Evaluate Select	Your sales presentation wins	Give yardsticks
Purchase	Offer is easy to say 'yes' to Unthreatening	Clear contract terms
Monitor	All positive	Feedback Build relationship

that size – we offer a three year warranty on these', 'The ones here also offer a sofa bed. Do you want a sofa bed?' etc. Again during a first store visit:

- Make customers a sales offer before they leave, with a deadline on a product that seems to match their needs.
- Give customers yardsticks by which they can measure competitor products: 'Remember we offer free delivery and for this week only, products to protect against stains at no extra cost'.
- Provide customers with a point of contact (perhaps a telephone number).
- Give customers literature about the product and directions to competitors' stores.

At the appropriate point when a sales opportunity has been reached (as the table shows), the sales presentation runs through the customers' needs, describing and demonstrating how the product matches each need. Then it is easy to close the sale.

As a retailer you should allow suppliers to train your sales staff in their products to give them the knowledge they need to sell on your behalf. In-house trainers have other priorities (like health and safety, company security

Table 19.2 The sales process

Point in the buying process	Objective	Practical steps
Potential buyer has just become aware of you or your company	Build relationship Fact find Qualify	Deliver evidence of the six Cs Start relationship
Potential buyer is aware of you but not a customer or client	Obtain a sales opportunity	Keep in contact Contact plan Put across offer as matched benefits Match case studies
Potential buyer represents a sales opportunity	Make a sales presentation Win a contract or sale	Find any project and each buyer's needs prior to presentation
Becomes a client offer	Demonstrate correct purchase or contract award made	Obtain feedback on performance

and till procedures) and may also not be fully trained in the suppliers' products.

If you are a supplier then, as indicated above, it will certainly pay dividends if you take the time to train the sales staff of the clients you supply about the features and benefits of your products, your POS and the situations in which customers can use them to best effect. People seem to have little imagination and need to envisage how products will benefit them. Sales staff, if they have a modicum of enthusiasm, soak up such training – as they do get asked about products and will want to respond appropriately. This may help them to steer customers to a sale of your products in preference to a competitor's. Not many suppliers consider offering sales training to their client retail outlets. Which is of course why FM staff are so excellent as it is accepted as part of their remit.

Should you wish to go part way and train your in-house staff in sales there is a solution. A professional chartered marketer will not need long to establish from market research the offer, brand values and the buying process from which a sales process is constructed. By way of example, one of the authors finds that for clients of smaller businesses this can be achieved in about five days of work for non-consumer products.

Remember, once you have tried out any of the suggestions above you will realize just how valuable effective selling is. That is the time to consider outsourcing sales to the professionals. Try a short-term project first.

Improving selling to B2B and B2P customers

Buyers are met through visits to their companies or at trade shows and exhibitions (see below). Just occasionally they make a visit to the suppliers to see for themselves. The role of influencers on the buyer touched on in Chapter 1 is really important. Here the value of a brand is important. A B2B company needs a brand just as much as a retail outlet. The brand does not have to be universal, but be known to clients and sufficient potential clients to satisfy any sales targets, any influencers and the respective trade media. Building a brand is a task for a chartered marketer and outside the scope of this book. The purpose here is to cover the face-to-face encounters and see if there are improvements to be made. There are still some lovely buyers that only believe they have done their job if they achieve a 10 per cent discount for their company. They are hardened to any other ploy. So in these days of print capability it is possible to accommodate this need and produce an appropriate price list and allow them their 10 per cent off.

A buyer face-to-face on a supplier's premises

Dealing first with the visit of a buyer to a supplier; it may be by invitation, it may be unexpected – but the supplier should have a routine established for a buyer's visit. A quick alert by telephone should prepare all for the visit. It is a golden opportunity to sell in to the buyer: as they are taken round the premises from department to department meeting people, the quality and benefits of the product can be shown in the way it is designed and manufactured and also how it is delivered and the after-sales service applied. In fact it should bring to life the offer – the 6Cs. Building relationships in B2B is just as important as for B2C. A visit can be enhanced through having photographs of products in use, placed in appropriate positions, or examples of all the alternative production capabilities adjacent to the machines that make them. As a part of in-house staff training in marketing, the purpose of visits to a company should be explained. Training a whole firm in marketing pays real sales dividends. In one of the authors' clients, sales did not fall as seasonally expected in the winter of 2006–2007 but remained at their summer high level as a result of the impact of marketing training.

Face-to-face meetings at a buyer's premises

A supplier visit to a buyer must stem from knowledge. This includes knowledge in detail about your own company's products, about the client company and its needs for the products and the people involved with the buying decision. All facts and figures relating to previous and forecast sales and any forecasts of future sales should be known. A sales process analysis will indicate what stage the buyer is at. A new buyer has to be taken through the stages. Detailed notes should be taken of the face-to-face meeting and circulated to anyone involved with the buyer or the buyer's company. Within the buyer firm the person who is representing the supplier will be seen as the embodiment of the brand and the type of the relationship established will be noted.

The 'marigold glove' theory of B2B sales relationships applies to whom in a buyer's company should be involved. The analogy is that when two marigold gloves are linked with fingers interlocking they are difficult to separate; so it is with two businesses, supplier and buyer, if the arrangement has been fully set up. At each level a link is established from managing director or CEO downwards. It makes doing business easier as the influencers can be made aware of the supplier's brand throughout the buyer's company. It makes it easier for the buyer to buy from the supplier. It is also harder to terminate a relationship between such multi-linked firms. (Better the devil you all know ...).

Professional face-to-face situations

A key element in face-to-face professional presentations for a contract pitch is to win. All that work goes to waste if any other result is achieved. In addition to knowledge and the ability to demonstrate technical, financial, management and team building competence, the individual needs of those around the table assessing the pitches and deciding the winner must be known and their needs covered in the face-to-face pitch meeting. The ability to communicate these competences in a self-effacing way is also important among professionals.

Case study: The value of knowledge

As a result of market research for an office removals company (about 10 per cent of blue-chip firms move offices each year) it was discovered that office managers had a widely held secret fear. The team of salesman could win a pitch once they reached the final firms chosen to pitch (typically five firms). Their problem was getting through the 50 firms invited for selection. Once trained in the secret fear they were able to confirm in their face-to-face 'selection to the 50' meeting with the office manager, that it was a real problem they could resolve. They proceeded to the final stage which they usually won. It added 22 per cent to the bottom line at a stroke.

Case study: Winning face-to-face professional presentations

Training in presentational skills, establishing a knowledge database of previous projects and developing a brand, took a firm from 'in the noise' to a position of one of the top three firms in their part of a UK construction sector. The key was winning at least 50 per cent of face-to-face presentations when pitching for projects, often from a field of six without dropping the price (the company was typically the second or third most expensive of the six).

Case study: A sales visit disaster

Accompanying, at the behest of the owners, an incentives salesman to the UK office of a French (Paris-based) casserole maker it was apparent that the salesman had done no homework. He had no idea about casseroles. He had no idea about the Paris base nor that that was where employees were trained. The fact that the firm employed a workforce of nearly all mature women had also escaped him. His incentive offer was to take the best employees for a binge drinking weekend to Paris. Despite a brilliant presenter, which showed how powerful incentives can be, which he did not use until too late, he was ushered out of the office and a short while later out of his job, after confessing to a trail of unprepared face-to-face sales meetings.

Case study: An exceptional IT salesman

A Bill of Quantities software salesman arranged his audience (a building firm) carefully in front of him noting their names and jobs. He sat in front with a computer and his company's software behind him (it could produce a bill of quantities for a detached house in about an hour). With his presenter upside down across his knees (he had made a special knee clip),he started by asking how those present currently did the job. He asked each person to give an example of a problem he or she presently faced in the process. He made notes as they spoke. After that he showed them how you produce a bill of quantities using both his computer and the presenter, including as he went along addressing the individual problems raised. He summarized all this at the end and asked for questions – but for each individual he had effectively made the sale, personally, face-to-face.

Face-to-face at exhibitions and trade fairs

An exhibition is usually held separately for the trade and for consumers. Sometimes there are trade-only days within a mixed exhibition. The difference is important in that the contact time is considerably different between the two types; typically of the order of one or two minutes' contact time only for customers – usually consumers – as against the trade, where typical contact time may be around 20 minutes. When Autotech, the trade exhibition for the motor industry, was first organized manufacturers and suppliers assumed that the motor show parameters applied – stands filled with attractive scantily clad women dishing out glossy brochures. This did not meet the need for consultation. So a compromise was devised. Now Autotech stands are staffed by women professionals who are bright, chartered engineers with a full understanding of the highly technical products and capable of discussing engineering technical matters for hours if needed.

Selling products is not allowed at exhibitions (for security among other reasons) but taking orders is often the key purpose. Exhibitions are generally held by trade and by category. Sometimes a number of categories are combined and held simultaneously such as for the spring and autumn fairs held at the NEC. An example of a single category exhibition is the toy trade fair held at the end of January, now at the Excel site in Docklands. The UK Toy Fair is one of four international toy fairs closely linked by succeeding dates when toys for the following year, but principally for Christmas, are displayed and orders taken.

Sometimes the majority of order taking for some categories is carried out at an exhibition – the early February Spring Fair is when most purchasing of calendars for the following year takes place. A new company selling calendars to the retail trade in the UK may only be able to find buyers prepared to order calendars at that exhibition almost to the exclusion of the rest of the year – with any ongoing sales sold to the same designs through merchandisers. The corollary is that to sell calendars widely in the UK will require attendance, with a stand, at the trade fair to take orders.

Exhibition selection

For every category there are one or more exhibitions held. To find out what exhibitions are held and where, refer to specialist exhibition trade guides. The trade magazines and exhibition venues also list exhibitions held.

An exhibition can allow customers to handle, view, experience, sample, test, try, ask questions about and place orders for products and services. Careful selection of the exhibition (by category and trade) should ensure that plenty of the target market for your concept – products and services – will be attending. This does not mean that they will visit your stand or place orders – even if they have done so previously.

Stand design to match objectives

The design of the stand requires an understanding of the objectives set for attendance at the exhibition. The size and location within the exhibition area is important to consider as is the stand staffing to cope with expected numbers. It is better to start small and learn from experience when considering stand size. If a part of the purpose is to understand customers' problems in detail and discuss possible product or service solutions then it may be important to include an area where there are limited distractions and a degree of perceived confidentiality is possible. Staff at Helmsmen Business Consultants (Roddy Mullin's company) have found a particular design of booth works very well. This both hides and 'traps' the prospect, minimizes distractions and is relatively soundproof, yet allows an eye to be kept on the remainder of the stand by the stand person talking to the prospect. The booth has a small footprint.

It is a good idea if many brief discussions are likely to be required with prospective customers to seat those staffing that part of the stand on seats that place them at eye level with customers. This avoids fatigue. People are unhappy talking up or down to each other, preferring near horizontal eye contact. Areas of stand visible down aisles should have lettering large enough to be read at a distance with short crisp messages putting across concept benefits as 'attention getters'.

B2B face-to-face operation of an exhibition stand

As a generalization based on observation both from attendance and stand staffing over many years most people on exhibition stands have received little or inappropriate training to 'sell' at exhibitions. Training can enhance the sales performance several times (Helmsmen' clients have increased order taking by a factor of 3 or 4 after training – the selling process at exhibitions is covered in the table below. It is different from the normal sales process in that you need to ascertain whom is in front of you first – owner, buyer or runner. (A runner is sent round by the buyer to look at stands they are not visiting). Training should be designed to impart an understanding of the alternative types of customer visiting the stand and the sales process to match those types – again described earlier in this book. The operation also varies according to the product or service.

It can be very useful to convert the exhibition sales process into a question tree script.

Tips

- Before you set out, test the script that will be used by your stand team on colleagues.
- Have a series of opening remarks and change them daily.
- Meet people outside the stand boundary, not just on the stand.
- Give stand staff a break every hour.

Table 19.3 The exhibition sales process

Point in the buying process	Objective	Practical steps
Potential buyer has just become aware of your brand and concepts	Qualify Fact find Build relationship Make offer open to the end of that day or the show – if you are the first stand visited Send the potential buyer to your competitors Ascertain the buyer type – owner, buyer or runner	Open with non-threatening dialogue – with everyone Deliver evidence of the six Cs Ask questions Qualify: if the person is an owner, test close if the person is a runner, offer all literature
Potential buyer is aware but not a customer	A sales opportunity – test close	Deliver evidence of the six Cs
Potential buyer represents a sales opportunity	Win the sale	Find the buyer's needs Close the sale
Becomes a customer	Demonstrate previously correct purchase occurred Show new items Close the sale	Obtain feedback on offer performance Keep in contact Contact plan Put across matched benefits

- Visit competitors' stands to see how they are doing and how they do it.
- Use a bar code reader as well as collecting business cards.
- Take information on every stand visitor and staple their card to their enquiry sheet.
- Load up the runner with every brochure you have.
- If you have an owner visit you should aim to take an order – owners have the power.
- Change the stand messages two or three times a day.
- Have an 'Oh really' story for the press or media when they visit.
- Have something moving on the stand.
- Have something that is fun on the stand, but it must match the brand values.

An exhibition should be part of an integrated marketing activities campaign with advertising, PR and direct contact marketing activities planned alongside both sequentially and concurrently.

Summary

This chapter is designed to trigger thoughts about how good your staff are at sales and to offer guidance towards improvements. Selling as a generality is poorly carried out. If the in-house staff's natural talents and skills do not encompass sales, then consider out-sourcing the sales function to an FM agency. Trial a small task first then go for it. Application of the principles applied in FM disciplines in-house will demonstrate to an extent how effective a full outsourcing to an FM agency might be.

Self-study questions

19.1. What improving face-to-face measures can you put in place in-house?
19.2. What are the buyer process stages?
19.3. Describe the sales process practical steps to take at each stage.

(Answers can be found in the text.)

Further information

Useful organizations

Trade associations

Advertising Standards Authority (ASA) and Code of Advertising Practice
Committee (CAP)
Mid City Place
71 High Street
Holborn
London WC1V 7QT
Tel: 0207 492 2222
e-mail: mattw@asa.org.uk
www.asa.org.uk
Offers copy advice by e-mail.

CAP's copy advice service:
Tel: 0207 580 4100
Fax: 0207 580 4072
www.cap.org.uk
Offers advice online, plus related cases.

British Promotional Merchandise Association
Bank Chambers
15 High Street
Byfleet
Surrey KT14 7QH
Tel: 0207 689 5555
e-mail: susan@bpma.co.uk
www.bpma.co.uk
Has a list of members' products and services.

CAM Foundation
Moor Hall
Cookham
Maidenhead
Berkshire SL6 9QH
Tel: 01628 427192
Fax: 01628 427399
e-mail: mariagarcia@camfoundation.com
www.camfoundation.com
Covers specific areas of marketing communication and promotional aspects
of marketing for those pursuing a career in advertising, PR, media, market
research, direct marketing or sales promotion through examinations.

Chartered Institute of Marketing
Moor Hall
Cookham
Maidenhead
Berkshire SL6 9QH
Tel: 01628 427500
www.cim.co.uk
The home of the professional practitioner in marketing. Offer training
courses on most marketing subjects.

Chartered Institute of Purchasing and Supply
Easton House
Easton on the Hill
Stamford
Lincolnshire PE9 3NZ
Tel: 01780 756777
Fax: 01780 751610
e-mail: info@cips.org
www.cips.org

Direct Marketing Association
70 Margaret Street
London W1W 8SF
Tel: 0207 291 3338
Fax: 0207 291 3301
e-mail: info@dma.org.uk
www.dma.org.uk
The Direct Marketing Association (DMA) is Europe's largest trade association in the marketing and communications sector, with over 900 corporate members. On behalf of its membership, the DMA promotes best practice and self-regulation, through its codes, in order to maintain and enhance consumers' trust and confidence in the direct marketing industry. The DMA has set up the Direct Marketing Authority as an independent body to monitor industry compliance. The DMA offers an extensive range of assistance on its website, including codes of practice.

The Field Marketing Council
70 Margaret Street
London W1W 8SF
Tel: 0207 291 3300
Fax: 0207 291 3301
e-mail: info@dma.org .uk
www.dma.org.uk
The FMC is the trade body for the FM Industry, and is one of the councils within the DMA. The FMC is committed to improving standards within the industry, and promoting the discipline throughout the UK. Currently the FMC is chaired by one of the authors of this book.

Incorporated Society of British Advertisers (ISBA)
44 Hertford Street
London W1J 7AA
Tel: 0207 291 9020
Fax: 0207 629 5355
e-mail: alexr@isba.org.uk
www.isba.org.uk

Trade association for advertisers

Institute of Practitioners in Advertising (IPA)
4 Belgrave Square
London SW1X 8QS
Tel: 0207 235 7020
Fax 0207 245 9904
e-mail: rasdall@ipa.co.uk
www.ipa.co.uk
Getting into advertising is not easy. But we also know what a great career it can be. So for those of you who really want to know more, the IPA can give you a better understanding of what it is like to work in the advertising world, the variety of jobs that exist, what sort of skills you will need (and what you will learn), how to go about getting into the industry and which agencies are actively looking for graduates. The IPA is the trade body and professional institute for leading agencies in the UK's advertising, media and marketing communications industry.

Institute of Sales Promotion (ISP)
Arena House
66–68 Pentonville Road
London N1 9HS
Tel: 0207 837 5340
Fax: 0207 837 5326
e-mail: enquiries@isp.org.uk
www.isp.org.uk
The website has a 'Display' site containing nearly 200 examples of award winning promotions showing the market background, mechanics used and results. Coupon guidelines and checklists for promotional mechanics are also available. The ISP's purpose is to protect and promote professional and effective sales promotion. It provides professional qualifications at all levels. 'The ISP when promoting sales is your business'.

The Voucher Association (VA)
Contact: Andrew Johnson
Tel: 0870 241 6445
www.the-va.co.uk
The VA was established as a trade body in 1996 to represent the key players in the £3 billion corporate incentive and consumer gift voucher, card and stored value market. Today the association is known as The VA and has 56 issuer and service members and five social members, representing many of the key players in the industry.

Agency that supplied case studies

The FDS Group of Companies
Service and Field Marketing Agency of the Year – *The Grocer* 2005
Winners of 'Making it Happen' Award 2004 – BPMA/ISP
Premier Winners – DMA Excellence Awards 2004
Best use of data – Field Marketing and Brand Experience Awards 2005

FDS House
94–104 John Wilson Park
Whitstable
Kent CT5 3QZ
Tel: 08450 741111
Fax: 08450 741112
e-mail: info@fds-uk.com
www.fds-uk.com
Recognized as a leading award winning agency. FDS has a track record of delivering FM solutions that focus on and deliver increased sales. FDS is a full service FM agency.

General

Consumers Association
2 Marylebone Road
London NW1 4DF
Tel 0207 486 5544
Fax 0207 770 7600
 e-mail which@which.net
www.which.net

National Consumer Council
20 Grosvenor Gardens
London SW1W 0DH
Tel: 0207 730 3469
Fax: 0207 730 0191
e-mail info@ncc.org.uk
www.ncc.org.uk

National Statistical Office
Press and Information Office
1 Drummond Gate
London SW1V 2QQ
Tel: 0207 233 9233
Fax: 0207 533 6261
www.statistics.gov.uk

Magazines

Field Marketing (Quarterly)
Frank Publishing
Yew Tree Studios
Stanford North
Ashford
TN25 6DH
Tel: 01303 813183
www.marketingchannel.co.uk

Marketing
174 Hammersmith Road
London W6 7JP
Tel: 0207 413 4150
Fax: 0207 413 4504
www.marketing.magazine.co.uk

Marketing Week
12–26 Lexington Street
London W1R 4HQ
Tel 0207 970 4000
Fax 0207 970 6721
www.marketing-week.co.uk

Data capture and reporting provider

Matador Intelligence
94–107 John Wilson Park
Whitstable
Kent CT5 3QZ
Support tel: 01227 773537 or 01227 776407
Sales tel: 01227 773538; Fax: 01227 363289

e-mail: info@matadorintelligence.com

www.matadorintelligence.com

Matador Intelligence is a data capture and reporting provider that developed the right specialist skills for the broad FM agency scene. Matador Intelligence provide an 'operational intelligence' service with tailored joined-up reporting and capture systems and services to ensure that FM stays ahead of clients' own capabilities and expectations for brands. The company provides its customers with the competitive advantage being gained by immediate access to information and by the ability to react to opportunities as they happen. One of Matador's key products is SWIFT, which allows instant data capture through a standard mobile phone and is ideal for any strategic and tactical activities (availability, distribution, visibility or space, compliance, etc).

Marketing Consultancy

Helmsmen Business Consultancy

9 Lawrence Mansions

Lordship Place

London SW3 5HU

Tel: 0207 352 3846

Fax: 0207 352 3846

e-mail: roddywpmullin@hotmail.com

Helmsmen Business Consultants establish bespoke teams of freelance consultants – experts in their field – to solve business problems. Operating since October 1990 clients have included governments, agencies, large and small companies and individuals across a broad range of sectors including start-ups, expansions, routine long-term marketing advice and M&A assessments. Projects start with market analysis.

Glossary of abbreviations

ABC = Audit Bureau of Circulations
AFM = area field manager
ASM = area sales manager
B2B = business to business
B2C = business to consumer
B2P = business to persons
BSE = book stock errors
CEO = chief executive officer
CFO = chief financial officer
Chartered marketer = marketing professional accorded status by the
                     Privy Council
CIPS = Chartered Institute of Procurement and Supply
CRM = customer relationship management
CTU = counter top units
DIY = do-it-yourself
DMA = Direct Marketing Association
EFMP = European Field Marketing Partners
EPOS = electronic point of sale
FDS = FM company owned by one of the authors
FM = field marketing
FMC = Field Marketing Council
FMCG = fast moving consumer goods
FSA = Financial Services Authority

FSDU	=	free standing display unit
FSE	=	field service executive
Google	=	internet search engine
HHC	=	hand-held computers
HR	=	human resources
ICO	=	Information Commissioners Office
IiP	=	Investors in People
IMS	=	internal management system
ISP	=	Institute of Sales Promotion, also internet service provider
KPI	=	key performance indicator
PDA	=	personal digital assistant
POP	=	point of purchase, used instead of POS
POS	=	point of sale
RFM	=	regional field manager
ROE	=	return on expenditure
ROI	=	return on investment
SEL	=	shelf edge labels
SKU	=	shelf keeping unit (i.e. a product)
SLA	=	service level agreement
SMART	=	specific, measurable, agreed, reasonable and time bound.
SMS	=	short message service
Tip-ons	=	vouchers stuck to the pages of magazines
TNS	=	Taylor Nelson Soffres
TPS	=	telephone preference service
USP	=	unique selling point
VAT	=	value added tax
WCM	=	Worshipful Company of Marketors
WKS	=	Willott Kingston Smith

References and further reading

Cummins, J and Mullin, R (2008) *Sales Promotion*, Kogan Page, London

Mullin, R (2001) *Value for Money Marketing*, Kogan Page, London

Parker, D (2006) The Year Ahead 2007, *Marketing Week*, [Online] http://www.marketingweek.co.uk/item/54446/pg_dtl_art_news/pg_hdr_art/pg_ftr_art

Royal Society of Arts (RSA) (1995) *Tomorrow's Company: The role of business in a changing world*, Gower, Aldershot

Underhill Paco (2003) *Why We Buy: The science of shopping*, Thomson Texere

The following are available for purchase or view on www.dma.org.uk, but cannot be downloaded or printed:

Users' Guide to Field Marketing

DMA Codes of Conduct

FMC Best Practice Guidelines

DMA Guide to Responsible Sampling

Index